D1393815

BEST-KEPT SECRETS OF
BARCELONA

Publisher and Creative Director: Nick Wells
Commissioning Editor: Polly Prior
Editorial Assistant: Taylor Bentley
Art Director: Mike Spender
Layout Design: Jane Ashley
Copy Editor: Anna Groves
Proofreader: Dawn Laker
Indexer: Helen Snaith

FLAME TREE PUBLISHING
6 Melbray Mews
London SW6 3NS
United Kingdom

www.flametreepublishing.com

First published 2019

19 21 23 22 20
1 3 5 7 9 10 8 6 4 2

© 2019 Flame Tree Publishing Ltd

All rights reserved. No part of this publication may be reproduced, stored in a retrieval system, or transmitted in any form or by any means, electronic, mechanical, photocopying, recording or otherwise, without the prior permission in writing of the publisher.

Every effort has been made to contact image copyright holders. We apologize in advance for any omissions and would be pleased to insert the appropriate acknowledgement in subsequent editions of this publication.

A CIP record for this book is available from the British Library upon request.

Photography by **Hugh Palmer** and © **Flame Tree Publishing Ltd**: 12, 14, 17, 18, 20, 21, 23, 24, 31, 44, 45, 48, 50, 51, 54, 56, 64, 82, 85, 86, 87, 94, 101, 104, 105, 106, 107, 111, 112, 116, 117, 119, 129, 139, 145, 146, 147, 153, 171, 182, 186, 187. Courtesy of **Shutterstock.com** and © the following contributors: 15 Paolo Fassoli; 16 Neirfy; 22 Takashi Images; 26, 58, 69, 168 Alessio Catelli; 27, 67, Mark52; 28 DaLiu; 30 Lipskiy; 32, 34, 72, 91, 127, 138, 178, ksl; 35 Mihai-Bogdan Lazar; 36 KarSol; 38, 160 Pajor Pawel; 42, 46, 57, 65, 70, 71, 108, 122, 123, 136, 144, 148, 170, 174, 175, 177, 180, 181, joan_bautista; 47, 120 Veniamin Kraskov; 53 Lisa A; 60 Jaroslav Moravcik; 61 Christian Mueller ; 62 ansharphoto; 66 Veronika Kovalenko; 73 Eugene Ivanoff; 74, 184 kavalenkava; 76 Phant; 78 Nejron Photo; 77 Oleg Proskurin; 80 gg-foto ; 81 Adriana Sta. Rosa; 83 TTstudio; 88 volkova natalia; 90, 163 Karol Kozlowski; 92 csp; 95 Rachel Graf; 96 saiko3p; 100, 162 Lena Serditova; 102 Mapics; 109 Shevchenko Andrey; 110 Meritxell Torne; 113 Tree_kangaroo; 114 J2R; 115 Studio Barcelona; 118 vvoe; 121 Beautiful landscape; 126 Karan Khurana; 128 Stefano Carnevali ; 130 tichr; 131 Brian Kinney; 132 Roka; 134 alionabirukova; 135 nito; 137 tomtsya; 140 photosil; 141 Anibal Trejo; 143 Ioan Panaite; 150 Saejun Ahn ; 155 Toniflap; 158 Anamaria Mejia; 159 Iakov Filimonov ; 165 Moarly; 166 Mariia Kan; 167 Marco Rubino; 172 OSORIOartist; 176 4kclips ; 183 Tono Balaguer; 188 Frank Bach. Courtesy of **SuperStock.com** and © the following contributors: 84 Jordi Sans / age fotostock; 151, 173 Alfred Abad / age fotostock; 154, 164 MAISANT Ludovic / hemis.fr / Hemis. Courtesy of **Getty Images** and © the following contributors: 68 Stefano Politi Markovina; 152 DEA PICTURE LIBRARY.

ISBN 978-1-78755-293-7

Printed in China | Created, Developed & Produced in the United Kingdom

BEST-KEPT SECRETS OF
BARCELONA

MICHAEL ROBINSON

**FLAME TREE
PUBLISHING**

CONTENTS

INTRODUCTION

If one types 'Barcelona' into an internet search engine, the city and the famous football team of the same name vie for top listing, so synonymous are the two. However, the football team's success is recent history, whereas the city has a cultural heritage that goes back over two thousand years, long before it was occupied by the Romans as part of its empire. Then it was known as Barcino, in what are now the Waterside area and the Barri Gòtic (Gothic Quarter). The Latinized name was from the ancient settlement of Barca, created by the Carthaginian general Hamilcar Barca (275–228 BC), father of Hannibal (247–c. 181 BC), one of the greatest military strategists of the ancient world. Today, one can still find remnants of the Roman wall that surrounded Barcino, some of which is incorporated into the cathedral walls, and the Roman grid system of roads is still evident in the Barri Gòtic.

Like much of Europe in the period after the Roman Empire, Barcelona was invaded by a Germanic tribe, in this case, the Visigoths, before being captured, firstly by the Arabs and then Charlemagne's son Louis the Pious (778–840) in 801. At this time, Barcelona became the centre of the Hispanic March, a military buffer zone between the warring factions of the Muslims, who occupied Southern Hispania (Spain), and the Frankish states to the north. The zone was controlled by successive counts of Barcelona from 801 until 1410, when the title ceased to be used, having been part of the Kingdom of Aragon since 1137. In the latter part of the fifteenth century, the kingdoms of Aragon and Castile became one with the marriage of Isabella of Castile (1451–1504) and Ferdinand II of Aragon (1452–1516), eventually leading to the creation of the Kingdom of Spain. They were also responsible – in 1492 – for ending the *Reconquista*, when the lands that had been occupied by the Muslims for the previous 700 years were retaken and Spain became totally Catholic.

Queen Isabella was also instrumental in funding and promoting the first voyage of Christopher Columbus (1451–1506) in 1492, opening the gateway to the Americas and the colonization of

much of South America. This marked the beginning of Spain as Europe's first superpower through conquest and trade. Columbus returned from his first voyage to the New World a hero and was greeted in Barcelona by the king and queen, despite the royal court being in Madrid. Six Native Americans, who accompanied Columbus on his return, were subsequently baptized in Barcelona Cathedral.

At the end of the fifteenth century, the evolution of the kingdom of Spain, with its court and political power now centred in Madrid, created a hiatus in the fortunes of Barcelona as a trading port. Spain was at that time much more interested in exploiting the New World's resources through conquest rather than trading with Europe.

Barcelona is the capital of Catalonia, an autonomous region of Spain, with limited self-governing powers, given as part of the Spanish Constitution of 1978. Recently, Catalonia has sought to extend those powers by declaring its independence from Spain, a bid that ultimately failed. The impetus for Catalonia's independence began during the Catalan Revolt of 1640, an aspect of the Franco-Spanish War, in which its northern territories were eventually ceded to France as part of the Treaty of the Pyrenees (1659). A few decades later, a unifying decree led to the suppression of the Catalan language in favour of Spanish, leading to further resentment on the part of the Catalans. The period from 1714 until the 1830s is often referred to as the *Decadència,* or the cultural decline of Catalonia.

In the nineteenth century, Catalonia, and in particular Barcelona, experienced significant industrialization, the wealth from

which spawned the *Renaixença* (Catalan Renaissance), a cultural revival of its customs, traditions and language. In the 1850s, the urban planner Ildefons Cerdà (1815–76) created the Eixample (Expansion) district of Barcelona, tearing down the city's medieval walls in the process, similar to the contemporaneous modernization of Paris by Baron Haussmann (1809–91). Like many European cities, Barcelona developed its own form of architecture and design at the end of the nineteenth century. This was driven by the need for design to reflect modernity, which was in a continuing state of flux, and often as a reaction

Barcelona continued to enjoy a cultural renaissance funded mainly by its industrial might until the calamitous events of the 1930s. Despite the *Generalitat* (Catalan government) being reinstated by the Spanish government following the declaration of the Second Republic in 1931, the city fell prey to anarchist groups. In 1939, at the end of the Spanish Civil War, the military dictator General Franco (1892–1975) seized power. This had a lasting effect not only on the city but on all Catalonia, which had its language and autonomy suppressed.

The death of Franco in 1975 and the awarding of the Summer Olympics to Barcelona for the 1992 Games facilitated a huge turnaround in the city's fortunes. In that time, Barcelona went from what was just a large industrial city to a European cultural centre that ranks in the top tier for visitors. The awarding of the Summer Olympics of 1992 to Barcelona was the most transformative event, which saw the razing of disused industrial units, warehousing and docklands and the creation of a two-mile stretch of golden beach. The sporting venues were sited across the city, but concentrated in the Montjuïc area (*see* page 125). The regeneration of the city into a Mediterranean coastal resort has today made Barcelona the fifth most popular tourist destination in Europe and twelfth in the world.

to the dominant academic styles of the previous decades. The resulting aesthetic has been variously called Art Nouveau in Paris and Brussels, *Jugendstil* in Germanic countries and *Sezessionstil* in Vienna. In Barcelona, it became known as *Modernisme*, or *Modernista*, a style that also reflected Catalan culture. Its main practitioners were Lluís Domènech i Montaner (1850–1923), who designed the Castell dels Tres Dragons, for the Barcelona Exposition of 1888; Josep Puig i Cadafalch (1867–1956); and of course the most eminent and prolific of them all, Antoni Gaudí (1852–1926), whose idiosyncratic style dominates the city of Barcelona, most notably at the church of the Sagrada Família (*see* page 102).

Today, Greater Barcelona is still an industrial hub; it is the location of the headquarters of the Seat car company and has a population in excess of three million inhabitants. Its GDP is nearly fifty per cent higher per capita than the European average and ranks as one of the top five business districts in Europe. The World Trade Centre in the Port Vell district of central Barcelona is its testimony (*see* page 20). However, like most European cities, its manufacturing has declined in recent years and has been overtaken by the services sector. The textile industry was, and still is, very important to the city, making it the fifth most important fashion capital, behind London, Paris, Milan and New York.

The seminal year for Barcelona's development was in 1986, when Spain became a member of the European Community. The following year, the city was divided into ten administrative districts: Ciutat Vella, the oldest part of the city that includes the Barri Gòtic, Port Vell (the old harbour), El Raval and Barceloneta; Eixample, the most densely populated part of the city and home to most of the *Modernista* buildings in the city; and Sants-Montjuïc, an area that was completely redeveloped in the twentieth century, firstly for the Barcelona Exposition of 1929 and then the Summer Olympics of 1992. To the west of the city are two more districts: Les Corts, the home of FC Barcelona; and Sarrià Sant-Gervasi, the second largest urban area after Sants-Montjuïc. To the north are two more, Gràcia, the smallest district by area and yet the second most densely populated; and Horta-Guinardó, which is surrounded by the hills of Collserola and has very hilly streets. The final three districts are to the east: Nou Barris, Sant Andreu and Sant Martí, the latter two being linked by the Bac de Roda Bridge (*see* page 175).

Barcelona is, however, greater than the sum of its geographical parts. It is not just a city with a fascinating history, which at times has been turbulent, but one that has a vibrant, forward-thinking culture that appeals to all age groups. It is virtually impossible to get bored in Barcelona, from the family activities at the Fundació Joan Miró (*see* page 134) to a concert at l'Auditori or the Gran Teatre del Liceu (*see* page 64); from a shopping spree in La Rambla (*see* page 54) to a quiet walk in the hills of Collserola, there is something for everyone. Barcelona never sleeps, its vibrant nightlife adding to the charms of this Mediterranean city. There are many bars and restaurants along the seafront suited to alfresco dining for most of the year. Most of the nightclubs are open until the small hours and can be found in the downtown areas, along with late-opening bars and restaurants.

This book is by no means a definitive guide to the city, and is unable to convey all that is exciting and enthralling about its place in history and as a cultural capital of the world. Its remit is to whet your appetite for a visit to this most enchanting place.

THE WATERFRONT

P ort Vell, literally the 'Old Harbour', is the waterfront area of Barcelona, from the Barceloneta area in the east to the statue of Columbus in the west, and in its heyday was a major European port. However, until the regeneration of the area prior to the 1992 Summer Olympics, this was an area of neglected warehouses. Today, it has 16 million visitors and is home to the Maremagnum, a shopping centre described as a 'sea of shops, restaurants and entertainment' because of its location, which is accessed across the quirky Rambla del Mar. Close by are the Golondrinas, a fleet of small boats that take tourists around the harbour on pleasure cruises.

At the other end of the waterfront is Barceloneta Market, an extraordinary building first built in 1884, and more recently remodelled by the young Spanish architect Josep Miàs (b. 1966), who has created a new light and airy internal space that enhances the shopping experience. The market was relocated and opened in 2007 with the intention of creating a new hub for the Barceloneta community. It has green credentials, in that one third of the energy used in the market by stallholders is created using solar panels integrated into the design.

BOATS IN HARBOUR

Port Vell

Port Vell has two marinas for pleasure craft. The Real Club Náutico de Barcelona, founded in the nineteenth century, operates many of the moorings used and is internationally renowned for the organization of competitive sailing regattas in the Mediterranean. A number of world- and European-class regattas take place in Barcelona each year. The larger or super yachts are normally catered for at another marina run by One Ocean.

THE OLD CUSTOMS HOUSE

Port Vell

The Old Customs House was designed by Enric Sagnier
(1858–1931) and built between 1896 and 1902. Its eclectic
style has its basis in Neoclassicism, but also anticipates the
Modernisme of the twentieth century through Art Nouveau.
The building was heavily ornamented by Sagnier to emphasize
the importance of its purpose. The towers at each end have
four winged sphinxes, reminiscent of those that guarded the
entrance to the ancient Greek city of Thebes. These creatures
played an important role in mythology, a subject very close to
the architect's heart.

MIRAESTELS

Port Vell

There are two pristine white figures made from fibreglass
and plastic floating in Port Vell Harbour. The figures are
staring towards the heavens as stargazers (*miraestels*) and were
designed by the Barcelona artist Robert Llimós (b. 1943). He
was inspired by a Joan Brossa (1919–98) poem that refers to a
person looking at the night sky as an allegory of humanity. The
figures were unveiled in 2010, having been commissioned by
the Barcelona Foundation for Ocean Sailing.

PAELLA

Port Vell

There are many restaurants along the shoreline of Barcelona, most of which cook freshly caught seafood. Paella, always considered a traditional Spanish dish, is originally from further down the coast at Valencia. Their version of paella uses rice and meat (traditionally chicken or rabbit), but in other areas such as Barcelona, it is more common to use seafood, such as prawns and mussels and occasionally lobster. It is also now quite common to cook mixed paella that uses both meat and seafood.

COLOM MONUMENT

Port Vell

After returning from his successful first voyage to the New World in 1493, the explorer Christopher Columbus arrived in Barcelona to a hero's welcome by King Ferdinand II and Queen Isabella. With him, Columbus brought back six Native Americans, who were baptized into the Christian faith at Barcelona Cathedral. Although Columbus never sailed directly to or from Barcelona, he still merits a monument as the founding father of the colonization of the Americas by the Spanish. The 60 m (200 ft) monument was designed as a centrepiece to the 1888 Barcelona Universal Exposition.

SANTA EULÀLIA SCHOONER AND MARITIME MUSEUM

Port Vell

The presence of the tall-mast schooner *Santa Eulàlia*, launched originally in 1918, reminds us that this was at one time the locality of the boat yards of Barcelona. After painstaking restoration, the ship, originally known as *Sayrernar Uno*, is moored at the Moll de la Fusta quay and renamed to honour Barcelona's patron saint. The boat yards were relocated in the eighteenth century, and in 1936, these medieval buildings were used to curate the maritime history of Catalonia. The museum has recently been completely refurbished and has a collection of pre-Columbian maps among its many artefacts.

RAMBLA DEL MAR

Port Vell

Although not a continuation of La Rambla itself, this walkway continues on the other side of the Plaça Portal de la Pau, linking the waterside to another spit of land known as the Moll d'Espanya. Popular with tourists, this wooden walkway opened in 1994. Here can be found one of Europe's largest aquariums and the shopping complex known as the Maremagnum, which is also home to the iMax cinema complex. In the background of the picture is the World Trade Centre and to the right is a tower, one of the staging points of the cable-car system across Port Vell.

LA PARELLA

Port Vell

The sculpture *La Parella* is of a couple sitting on the harbour wall in contemplative mood. Its artist is Chilean Lautaro Díaz Silva (b. 1953) and is a clear homage to Classical Greek sculpture that depicts limbless torsos, combined with the Romanticism of Auguste Rodin, a obvious influence. The sculpture is located at the former timber wharf, midway between the Columbus monument and the beach at Barceloneta. Seen from the other side, the couple's lower limbs, although human, have the appearance of a mermaid and a merman, as they contemplate the view across the ocean.

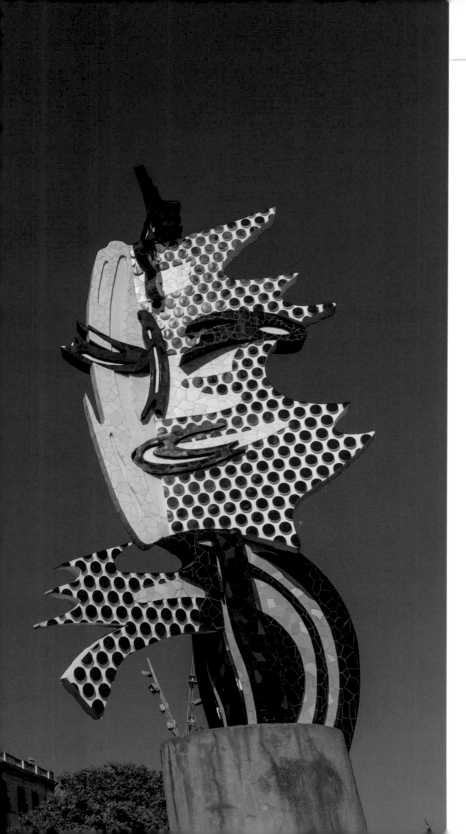

EL CAP DE BARCELONA

Port Vell

As part of the urban regeneration of the quayside for the 1992 Olympic Games, Pop artist Roy Lichtenstein (1923–97) was commissioned to create a three-dimensional image as a focal point for the area. Known as the 'Head of Barcelona', it is a rendition of the artist's more familiar two-dimensional works based on comic strips. It is made from concrete and mosaic in an obvious homage to the Catalan artist Antoni Gaudí. Although abstract, it is clearly a woman's head, the eyes heavy with mascara and the lips painted bright red.

SANTA MARIA DEL MAR

La Ribera

A magnificent fourteenth-century Gothic church, an example of medieval Catalan architecture, its façade is best seen under floodlight at night, which emphasizes the filigree stonework of the towers and the splendid rose window. The aisles either side of the nave are unusually narrow, which belies the broad appearance of the church from the outside. Another unusual feature of this Gothic church is the lack of transepts usually found in most European churches of this period. The church's interior was badly damaged in a fire in 1936, leaving it with little inside decoration.

PASSEIG DE JOAN DE BORBÓ

La Barceloneta

Referred to by the residents of Barcelona as the village within a city, the name literally means 'little Barcelona'. The area was built during the eighteenth century for the residents of La Ribera, who had been made homeless by King Philip V of Spain when he built the Ciutadella, a large fortress. The king created the citadel following the War of Spanish Succession (1701–14) and to maintain control over the city, preventing the Catalans from rebelling as they had in the previous century.

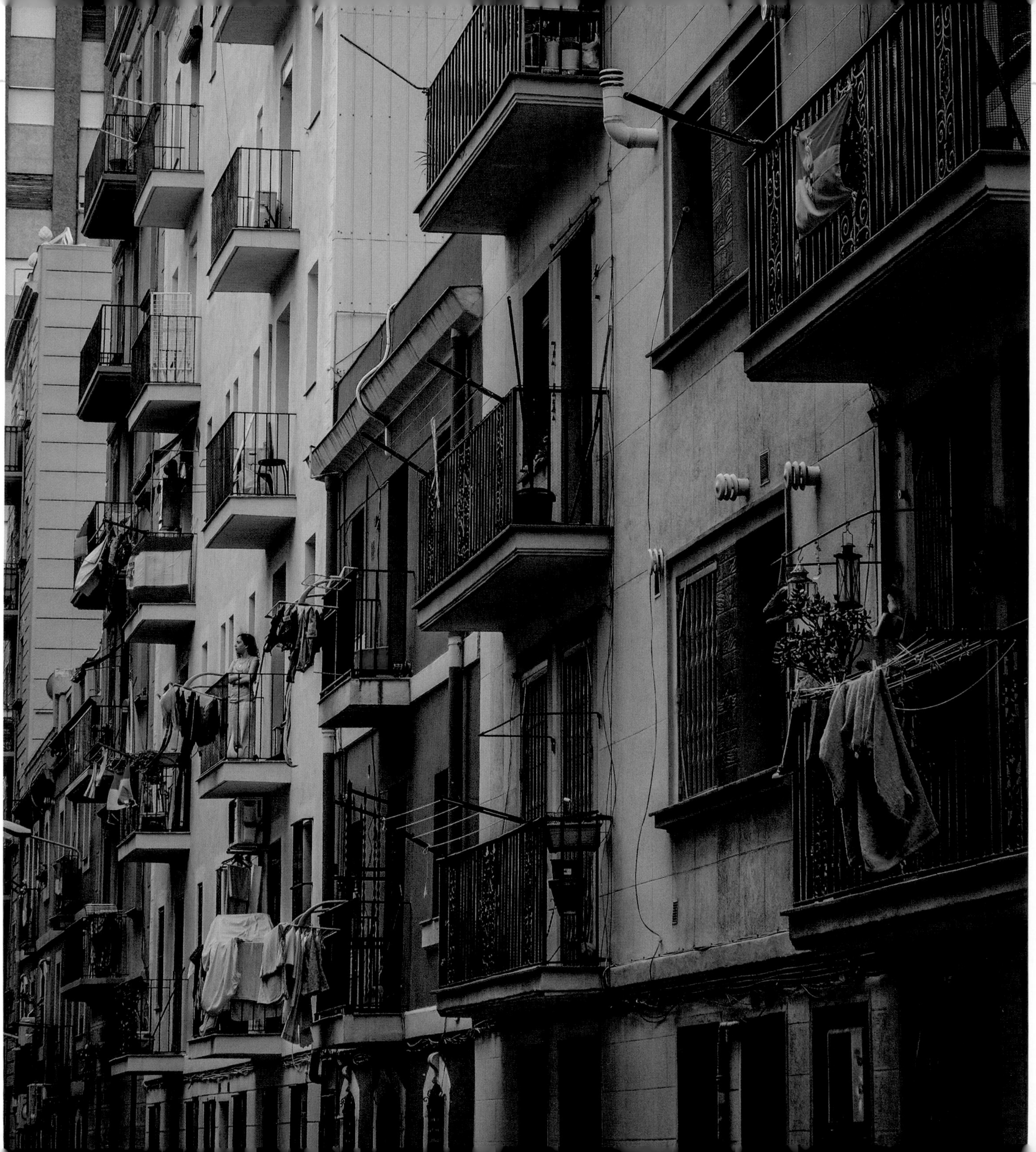

STREETS

La Barceloneta

The narrow grid system of streets in Barceloneta has created an intimate community of low-rise apartments, with many residents painting the walls of the houses in bright colours, emphasizing the Mediterranean climate and ambiance. Aside from offering a space in which to air clothes in the warm sun, the balconies provide an opportunity for displaying not only the Spanish flag but also the blue and yellow flag of La Barceloneta, an unusual parochial touch.

BARCELONETA MARKET

La Barceloneta

Originally built in the nineteenth century, the market had fallen into a state of disrepair before being refurbished by Josep Miàs, who kept the integrity of the iron and glass structure. The market has always been at the heart of this community, an aspect that the architect also wanted to retain. Unlike its predecessor, the market today has all the modern facilities and amenities that make for a highly pleasant shopping experience.

BARCELONETA BEACH

La Barceloneta

It is said that the magnificence of the beach at Barceloneta was the inspiration for the fictional chivalrous battle scene between Don Quixote and the Knight of the White Moon by the Spanish writer Miguel de Cervantes (1547–1616). Today, in the summer months, it is crowded with tourists seeking the lively atmosphere here during the day, through the evening and well into the small hours. It is very vibrant with many bars, restaurants and clubs, and an intriguing mix of old and new buildings such as the W Barcelona hotel at the end of the beach.

L'ESTEL FERIT

La Barceloneta

This 10 m (33 ft) sculpture called L'Estel Ferit (The Wounded Shooting Star) was created by the German artist Rebecca Horn (b. 1944) as part of the refurbishment, of the Barceloneta district in 1992, when the city was hosting the Olympic Games. As part of that refurbishment the city's authorities had destroyed the *xiringuitos*, a small shanty community of bars and restaurants contained within dilapidated shacks that were unsightly but popular with locals. The sculpture is Horn's tribute to the *xiringuitos*, its haphazard formation suggesting that it may topple at any given moment.

CAN SOLÉ

La Barceloneta

This Barceloneta fish restaurant has been in existence for over 100 years, a record it proudly boasts above its doorway and in its windows. Today, it does what it has always done – cooked fresh, locally caught fish. Originally, it was for the local fishermen and their families, but it is now one of the most respected seafood restaurants in Barcelona. On the walls of the dining area are many photos and drawings of and by its extensive clientele over the last century, including Joan Miró (1893–1983).

ESTACIÓ DE FRANÇA

La Barceloneta

As the name suggests, the station was originally constructed as the terminus for trains arriving from France. The original nineteenth-century building was rebuilt on a grander scale to the designs of Pedro Muguruza (1893–1952) and opened in 1929. It is often seen as one of the most superb examples of Neoclassicism, with decoration that spans the epoch of the Art Nouveau and Art Deco styles in a harmonious modern style. Muguruza later became one of the main architects for the Spanish dictator Francisco Franco.

PARC DE LA BARCELONETA

La Barceloneta

This park was newly created in 1996 on the site of an industrial complex that once contained an enormous gasometer and the offices of the municipal gas company. The building was designed by the Catalan architect Josep Domènech (1858–1917), who also created a water tower in a flamboyant Art Nouveau style that incorporates Moorish elements. Domènech is considered one of the pioneers of Modernisme in Barcelona. The water tower was recently refurbished, retaining much of its original eccentricity and charm.

PORT OLÍMPIC

Vila Olímpica

The marina at Port Olímpic was designed for the sailing events at the 1992 Olympics. Today, it functions as a marina, with over 700 berths. At the time of the development, the Casino de Barcelona was also created, which continues to function as a popular nightspot. Subsequent to the 1992 event, two large towers were constructed on the shoreline: an office complex known as the Torre Mapfre and the luxurious Hotel Arts, with its stunning views of the beach and the Mediterranean Sea.

EL PEIX D'OR

Vila Olímpica

Outside the Hotel Arts stands the enormous *El Peix d'Or*
(Golden Fish) by Frank Gehry (b. 1929). The sculpture
is over 50 m (164 ft) long and was commissioned for the
Olympics in 1992. At the time, before the hotel was built,
it stood in isolation along the shoreline, a reminder of the
fishing heritage of the area. The sculpture takes on different
appearances, depending on the weather and the brightness of
the sun, from a bright dazzling gold to a more sombre ochre
colour at sunset.

PLATJA DE LA NOVA ICÀRIA

Vila Olímpica

Close to the Port Olímpic is the lovely golden beach of the Nova Icària, a popular choice for families. It is also a venue used for several sporting activities, such as beach volleyball and table tennis. At the Port Olímpic end of the beach are several restaurants serving seafood. At the other end is the Espigó del Bogatell, a breakwater and jetty that leads to the longer Platja del Bogatell beach, used in the 1992 Olympic Games.

THE OLD TOWN

The Barri Gòtic (Gothic Quarter) is truly the heart of Barcelona, being the site chosen by the Romans for its administrative buildings. It has continued that function ever since, with the Casa de la Ciutat (City Hall) and the Palau de la Generalitat now in that location. Its thirteenth-century cathedral is on the site of a Roman temple. The Barri Gòtic is separated from the El Raval area by Barcelona's most famous street, La Rambla. The street, with its quirky shops and central market, is a must visit for any tourist to Barcelona.

El Raval was at one time the location of the city's red-light district because of its close proximity to the port, but today has a reputation as one of the city's hotspots for cosmopolitan food. The residential part of the quarter comprises a number of narrow streets. To the north-east of the Barri Gòtic are the areas known as La Ribera and El Born, housing the Picasso Museum and the fabulous Gothic church of Santa Maria del Mar. Equally fabulous is the Palau de la Música Catalana, a *Modernista* masterpiece by Domènech, with its extraordinary auditorium roof light.

STREETS

El Raval

The El Raval quarter is a truly cosmopolitan part of the city, made up of nearly 50 per cent émigrés, mainly from South America. More recently, it has attracted a large number of Eastern Europeans, taking advantage of the access through the European Union. Once considered a dangerous area, frequented by criminals and prostitutes, it was often referred to erroneously as 'Chinatown', despite not being inhabited by a Chinese community. Today, El Raval has the Museum of Contemporary Art and a plethora of restaurants and bars on its main streets.

MUSEU D'ART CONTEMPORANI

El Raval

The American architect Richard Meier (b. 1934) was commissioned to create a contemporary art space in 1989 despite there being no artworks to fill the galleries. Two years previously, two leading art critics were charged with founding the MACBA Foundation to look for suitable works and further develop the gallery. However, the museum did not open until 1995, missing the deadline of opening in time for the Olympic Games. These large Modernist buildings contrast very sharply with the narrow streets and houses of the neighbourhood.

CENTRE DE CULTURA CONTEMPORÀNIA DE BARCELONA

El Raval

The CCCB organizes seminars, exhibitions, festivals and concerts with the aim of exploring urban culture in the city. It is a public consortium run under the auspices of Barcelona City Council to create awareness and promote discussion with the public about the use of the city's resources and public spaces. The 15,000 sq m (161,458 sq ft) building houses a library, lecture halls and seminar rooms and of course exhibition spaces. The present building was opened in 1994 and occupies a site that was once a monastery and later a Jesuit seminary.

ANTIC HOSPITAL DE LA SANTA CREU

El Raval

Until the early twentieth century, this was the only hospital in Barcelona. It was housed in an early sixteenth-century building. By the end of the nineteenth century, it was apparent that the medieval buildings were no longer fit for purpose and a new facility, the Hospital de la Santa Creu i Sant Pau, was opened in the Eixample district in northern Barcelona. The old building now houses the Biblioteca Nacional de Catalunya (since 1939) and the Institute of Catalan studies, as well as two public libraries.

EL GATO DE BOTERO

El Raval

At the end of the Rambla del Raval is a huge sculpture of a cat, created by the Columbian artist Fernando Botero (b. 1932). Botero specializes in animal and female human forms on a large scale, having been influenced by Baroque art. The sculpture was purchased by the city council in 1987 and had a peripatetic life until being finally sited at its present location in 2003. There is another Botero sculpture of a horse at Barcelona airport.

RAMBLA DEL RAVAL

El Raval

The ramblas of Barcelona are the equivalent of the boulevards in Paris, wide avenues for walking, window-shopping and of course drinking and eating in the many bars and cafés. The Rambla del Raval is the newest of these, opened in 1995, which, like the Parisian boulevards, was created to gentrify the area that was until then somewhat down at heel. Far from displacing the residents, the Rambla del Raval invites the social inclusion of those most disadvantaged and is used for a variety of cultural events.

MONESTIR DE SANT PAU DEL CAMP

El Raval

The name of the monastery, 'St Paul in the Fields', belies the fact that it is now in central Barcelona, but until the fourteenth century, it was outside the city walls. It was originally a tenth-century church, later sacked by the Muslim warrior Almanzor (*c.* 938–1002) in 985, after which it was all but abandoned. Restorations were carried out in the twelfth century, when a new monastic order arrived, staying until the nineteenth century when the monasteries were secularized and the properties confiscated. The church was declared a national monument shortly after its closure.

LONDON BAR

El Raval

The London Bar has been a popular haunt since it opened in 1910, frequented by artists and writers such as Pablo Picasso (1881–1973) and Ernest Hemingway (1899–1961). The venue resembles a Victorian English pub or gin palace, that were once very popular in major cities such as London, their ornate, colourful interiors acting as a foil to the drab and dirty surroundings of the streets. The decoration usually consisted of elaborate illumination using chandeliers and an extensive use of mirrors and glass to reflect the light, making them inviting from outside.

DOORWAY, PALAU GÜELL

El Raval

One of the earliest Gaudí buildings, Palau Güell is located on La Rambla, completed in 1888, and is now one of the UNESCO World Heritage sites within the canon of Antoni Gaudí. The house was designed for the industrialist Eusebi Güell (1846–1918) to lavishly entertain high-society guests. Guests arriving by carriage at the unusual parabolic-shaped gates would then ascend a lavishly decorated staircase into the main function room with its high ceiling and perforations, illuminated to resemble the night sky.

CHIMNEYS, PALAU GÜELL

El Raval

The industrialist and entrepreneur Eusebi Güell was considered Gaudí's greatest patron. When Gaudí stated that it seemed only he and his patron loved the work, Güell famously stated that he did not like it, but respected it! He met Gaudí at the Paris World Fair in 1878, having seen the architect's work at the Spanish Pavilion. A utilitarian object such as a chimney in any other designer's hands would be just that; however, Gaudí was the master of architectural fantasy and used these objects to display his talents for decorative mosaic work.

LA RAMBLA

Las Ramblas

One of the most famous streets in Europe, La Rambla (also known as Las Ramblas) is a pedestrianized walkway that stretches from La Colom monument in Port Vell to the Plaça de Catalunya, dissecting the Barri Gòtic district to the east and El Raval to the west. In medieval times, the street was considered the centre of Barcelona life and was used for festivals and markets. At the beginning of the eighteenth century, trees were planted along its route, a feature that still exists today.

CASA BRUNO CUADROS

Las Ramblas

Known to the locals as the 'House of Umbrellas', the Casa Bruno Cuadros was designed by the architect Josep Vilaseca i Casanovas (1848–1910) in 1883 and is an early example of Catalan Modernisme, a version of Art Nouveau that was gaining in popularity at this time. Originally, the lower premises were used as an umbrella shop, the decoration and ornamentation above the door and on the façade providing evidence of its previous incarnation. Other decorative features include a dragon, enamelled glass and painted reliefs, Oriental motifs that were becoming popular in Western Europe.

ANTIGUA CASA FIGUERAS

Las Ramblas

Many wonderful examples of Art Nouveau styling, using curvilinear forms in the archaic lettering and stylized flora and fauna, can be found in the plethora of shops along La Rambla. Key features of the style include stained glass and an extensive use of mosaic work. This building was decorated by Antoni Ros i Güell (1877–1958) in 1902 and was formerly a pasta factory. On the corner of the building is a decorative relief panel of a woman harvesting wheat, by the sculptor Lambert Escaler (1874–1957), a homage to the original purpose of the building.

PLAÇA DEL PI

Las Ramblas

Located just off La Rambla is the Plaça del Pi, dominated on one side by the church of Santa Maria del Pi. The 'Square of the Pine' is so called because at one time, there was a pine tree at its centre. This has now been removed to reveal a number of fine decorative façades, behind which are many traditional shops and old bars and restaurants that have outside seating. Just off the square is the Carrer de Petritxol, a very narrow street with many interesting shops and small galleries.

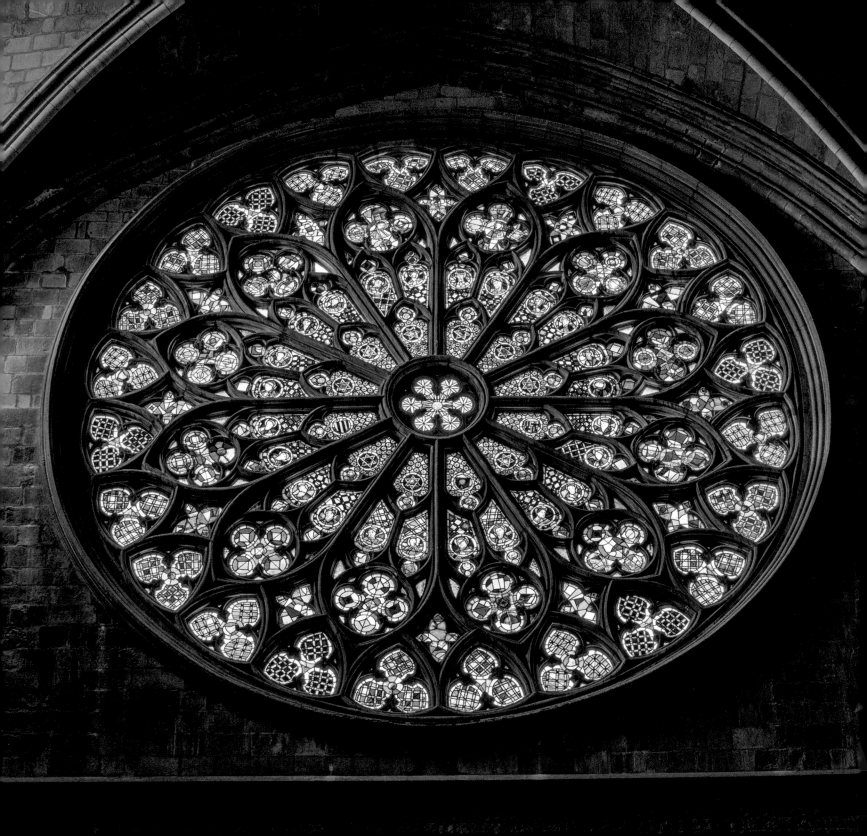

SANTA MARIA DEL PI

Las Ramblas

The basilica church with its separate campanile dominates one side of the Plaça del Pi, most notably with its huge rose window. The church dates from the fourteenth century, but the rose window is a replacement, the original destroyed in a fire in 1936 started by anarchists who sought to destroy the entire building. There had already been damage to the medieval building, most notably during the Catalonia earthquake of 1428 and during the War of Spanish Succession in the eighteenth century, when the altar and presbytery were destroyed.

MERCAT DE BOQUERIA

Las Ramblas

The first documentation of the existence of this market dates from the thirteenth century, when it sold meat. Gradually, the market expanded, with local farmers setting up stalls selling their own produce. The market was not formalized until 1827, when it had 200 stalls selling meat, fish and other produce. Following the destruction of the Convent of St Joseph after the secularization of the monasteries in 1837, the land was allocated to the stallholders to establish a covered market on the site.

EL MOSAIC DEL PLA DE L'OS

Las Ramblas

Close to the Plaça de la Boqueria, where the market is situated,
and in the middle of the walkway of La Rambla is a mosaic set
into the pavement called *Pla de l'Os* (The Plain of the Bone). By
the Catalan artist Joan Miró, it was created in 1976 and marks
the spot where the original Boqueria gate stood. Miró's works
are often described as childlike in their simplistic colourful
abstract forms, as demonstrated here. It is fitting that one of his
works is sited here, close to where he grew up in the Barri Gòtic
area of Barcelona.

GRAN TEATRE DEL LICEU

Las Ramblas

Known simply as Liceu, this opera house opened its doors in 1847 and was at the time the largest such venue in Europe, with a capacity of 3,500. The theatre was, however, almost completely destroyed in a fire in 1861, except for the façade and foyer, which were rebuilt and reopened the following year. In 1893, terrorists detonated a bomb inside the auditorium, killing 20 and injuring many more. Worse was to come in 1994, when a more devastating fire than the first in 1861 completely destroyed the theatre, which was subsequently rebuilt and opened in 1999 with improved facilities.

PLAÇA REIAL

Las Ramblas

On the Barri Gòtic side of La Rambla is a large square called Plaça Reial, which translates as 'Royal Plaza'. It is arguably the liveliest square in Barcelona, particularly at night, having a number of well-known nightclubs and bars. Each September, this is one of the many venues for the festival of La Mercè, observing the feast day of the Virgin Mary. Other celebrations occur here, such as those for New Year, and on Sundays, there is a stamp and coin market.

GAUDÍ STREET LAMPS, PLAÇA REIAL

Las Ramblas

The Plaça Reial has a number of palm trees to provide shade from the hot sun and has the Fountain of the Three Graces at its centre. There are also two street lamps that adorn the square, designed by a young Antoni Gaudí in 1879. These heavily decorated lanterns, surmounted by a winged helmet, are an indication of the ornateness of his later style. Despite the size of them, they cast a very sombre light in the evenings, which adds an ethereal dimension to the square.

LOS CARACOLES

Barri Gòtic

Los Caracoles is a restaurant renowned for its simple but excellent food, which it has been serving since 1835, when the Bofarull family founded it as Can Bofarull. The name was changed to its present one in homage to its signature dish of snails (*caracoles*), a typical Spanish dish often served as tapas. They are cooked in a broth made with herbs and spices, and served still in the shell. Once removed from the shell, they are eaten whole with the heads still on!

TAPAS AND SHERRY

Barri Gòtic

Tapas, meaning 'cover,' were pieces of bread or cheese used to cover a sherry glass to prevent insects getting at the contents. Tapas are now generally considered as snacks or appetizers of Spanish food, although in the last two decades or so, it has become a worldwide phenomenon. The snacks may be served hot or cold, and are often spicy, using chillies, garlic or paprika to enhance the flavours of the meat, fish or vegetable dishes. Sherry is a fortified wine made from white grapes usually grown in Andalucía.

STREETS

Barri Gòtic

The old narrow streets of the Barri Gòtic are alive with the hustle and bustle of daily life, the tourists visiting its diverse shops and being enchanted by the vibrant colours used to decorate the buildings. This is the heart of Barcelona, being the oldest part, where the Romans established their seat of government. Today, it is still the seat of the provincial government, which includes the fourteenth-century Casa de la Ciutat, or town hall. The central focus of the area is the Gothic cathedral of Santa Eulàlia.

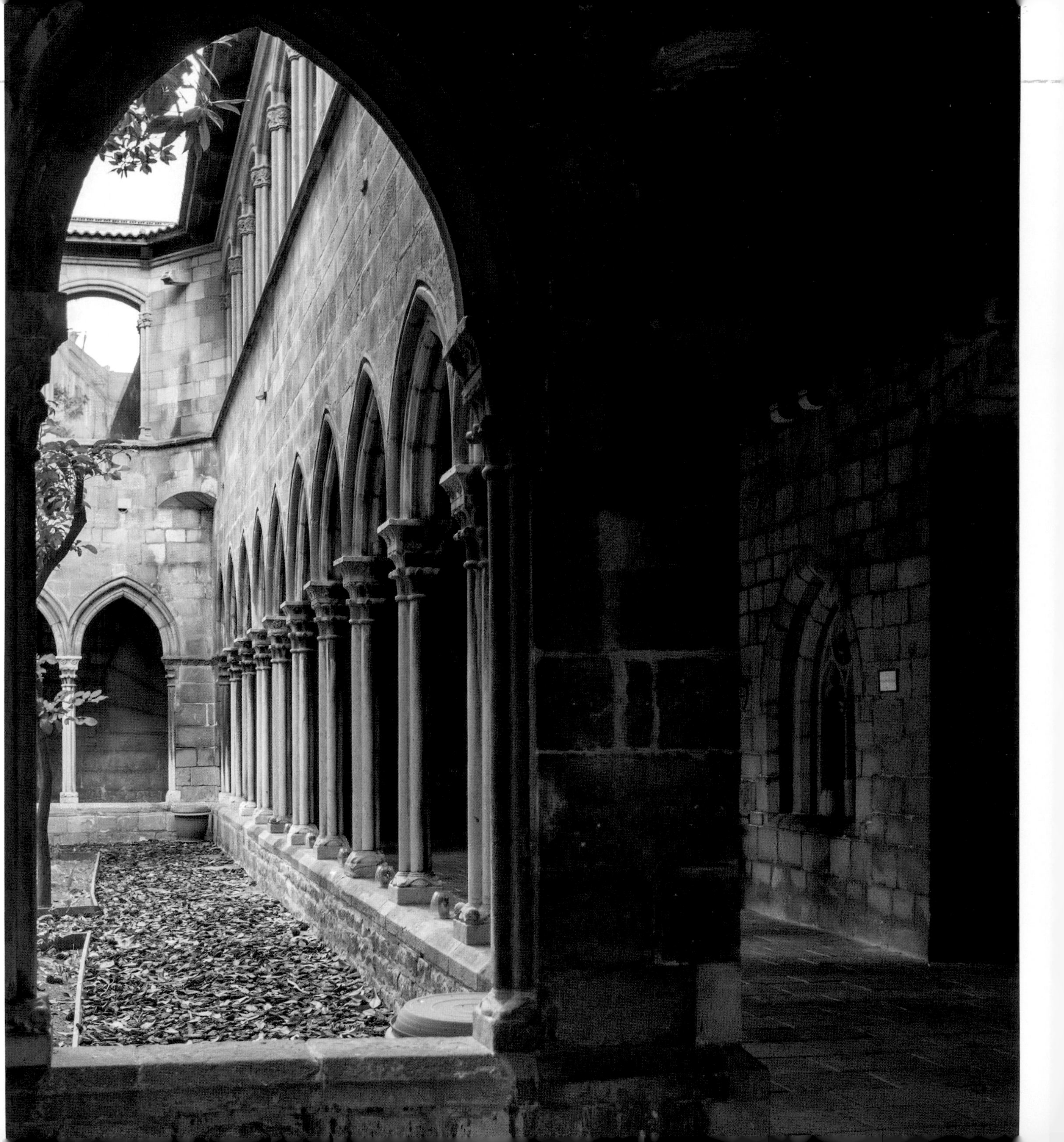

IGLESIA DE SANTA ANNA

Barri Gòtic

The church and former monastery of Santa Anna was originally created in the twelfth century and, although Romanesque in style, its layout is in the form of a Greek cross, with a short nave. Like all medieval monasteries, this was closed as part of the secularization of ecclesiastical buildings. The beautiful craftsmanship of medieval stonemasonry is still very much in evidence, and the venue provides a wonderful backdrop for concerts and recitals. The organizers also provide wine and sometimes dinner to enhance the visitor experience.

EL CALL

Barri Gòtic

Up until 1243, the Jewish community lived harmoniously with the other residents of medieval Barcelona, but the spread of anti-Semitism led to the Jews being forced to live in a ghetto, El Call, the Jewish Quarter. The ghetto was closed at the end of the fourteenth century, and less than one hundred years later, the Spanish Inquisition saw that the Jews were either expelled from Spain, murdered or forced to convert to Christianity, leading to their permanent exclusion in Spain until the 1920s.

MUSEU D'HISTÒRIA DE LA CIUTAT

Barri Gòtic

Within the medieval walls of the old royal palace is a museum of the history of Barcelona. It tells, for example, of the triumphal return of Columbus from the New World and his welcome by King Ferdinand and Queen Isabella in 1493, and of the council chamber of the Inquisition, both of which took place in the royal palace. The centrepiece of the museum is the maze of Roman streets in what was Barcino beneath the present streets of the old Barri Gòtic that can be explored by the public.

PALAU DEL LLOCTINENT

Barri Gòtic

Another building that is part of the royal palace complex is the Palau del Lloctinent, commissioned by the king (and Holy Roman Emperor) Charles V (1500–56) as the residence of his 'lieutenant' in Catalonia. Despite the palace being completed in 1549, it was not actually used as his residence, and until 1994, it contained the archive of the Crown of Aragon, covering the period from 1162 until its abolition in 1714, after the War of Spanish Succession. It was then moved to a building on Carrer dels Almogàvers. Outside of the palace is a magnificent courtyard with elements of Renaissance architecture, demonstrating the evolution of styles.

STATUE OF RAMON BERENGUER III

Barri Gòtic

This equestrian statue is of the twelfth-century Count of Barcelona, Ramon Berenguer III (1082–1131), who by conquest extended the lands of Catalonia beyond the Pyrenees. His subsequent marriage to the heiress of Provence ensured the continued expansion. Between them, they had seven children, who would later inherit the territories gained by their parents. In later life, Berenguer became a Templar Knight. The statue was designed in 1888 by the sculptor Josep Llimona (1864–1934), although the bronze figure was not actually cast until 1950.

FONT DE SANTA ANNA

Barri Gòtic

The oldest fountain in Barcelona is dedicated to St Anna and dates from 1356. Originally, it was octagonal in shape rather than the present hexagonal one and was totally refurbished in the early twentieth century, when the ceramic panels were added. They depict male and female figures together with stylized flora and fauna, typical of the Art Nouveau style. On the front of the fountain are the coat of arms of Barcelona and the year 1918 painted in Roman numerals. The tiles were designed and executed by Josep Aragay (1889–1973).

CLOISTER AT LE SEU

Barri Gòtic

The cathedral is dedicated to Santa Eulàlia (*c.* 290–303), a thirteen-year-old virgin tortured and murdered by the Romans, who were persecuting Christians under the orders of the Emperor Diocletian (244–311). It is said that she was tortured in thirteen different ways, including placing her in a barrel with knives fixed to the inside and rolling it down a hill. The cloister of the cathedral is home to thirteen live white geese which commemorate her martyrdom. Her remains are buried in the cathedral, together with a relief plaque depicting the martyrdom.

CATEDRAL DE SANTA EULÀLIA

Barri Gòtic

There has been a church on this site since the fourth century, the highest point in the old Roman city, which was destroyed by Almanzor in 985. By the end of that century, a new cathedral was planned by the Count of Barcelona, Ramon Berenguer I, built in the Romanesque style and consecrated in 1058. Just over two centuries later, the cathedral was rebuilt in the Gothic style, which we see today. The main façade of the church was added in the late nineteenth century. The church is often referred to simply as Le Seu.

THE THREE FRIEZES OF THE MEDITERRANEAN SEA

Barri Gòtic

Close to the cathedral, and in stark contrast, is the College of Architects of Catalonia, a Brutalist building constructed in 1955. The building is enlivened by a frieze designed by Pablo Picasso and installed in 1960. The frieze runs around three sides of the building. The work is actually etched into concrete panels by sandblasting to reveal the black layer beneath. It was executed by Norwegian sculptor Carl Nesjar (1920–2015) from Picasso's original drawings. The technique is known as Betograve and was used on several collaborations between the two artists.

PLAÇA DE SANT FELIP NERI

Barri Gòtic

This small square is dominated on one side by the church of Sant Felip Neri, dedicated to the Counter Reformist of the sixteenth century. The picture here reveals pockmarked walls, the result of two bombings during the Spanish Civil War in 1938. The first bomb killed 30 people, mostly children from the school next door, and as rescuers were seeking survivors in the rubble, a second bomb fell, killing another 12. Inside the square is an octagonal fountain, surrounded by Gothic buildings removed from other areas during modernization and re-erected here.

PLAÇA DE SANT JAUME

Barri Gòtic

At the centre of the old Roman city of Barcino is the Plaça de Sant Jaume, home to the administration of Barcelona. On one side of the square is the City Hall and on the other, the Palau de la Generalitat, the seat of the Catalonian government. The flags of Spain and Catalonia fly above the building, and it was as recently as 2017 that the Executive Council of Catalonia declared independence from Spain, causing a constitutional crisis. Having lost the subsequent snap election called by Spain's Prime Minister, the separatists went into exile.

BRIDGE, CARRER DEL BISBE

Barri Gòtic

The narrow lane known as the 'Bishop's Street' has an elaborate neo-Gothic bridge linking two buildings, the Casa dels Canonges and the Palau de la Generalitat. The street is medieval, the bridge having been added in 1928 by the architect Joan Rubió (1870–1952). Legend has it that Rubió incorporated a skull with a dagger inside, so that anyone who discovered it would be put under a curse. This macabre act was a retaliatory measure against the city's government, who had not sanctioned one of his larger schemes.

ROMAN WALLS,
PLAÇA TRAGINERS

Barri Gòtic

One of the best-preserved sections of the old Roman walls of Barcino can be found at the Plaça Traginers. This section is a defensive point at one of the corners of the wall and one of many examples of fourth-century Roman buildings to be found in Barcelona. A one-mile walk around the perimeter of the old city will reveal many such sites, some of which have a history that is at least three hundred years older than the Roman city.

AJUNTAMENT

Barri Gòtic

There has been a city council since the thirteenth century but the present Ajuntament (City Hall) building was not constructed until the beginning of the twentieth century and was added to in 1928. It was not, however, until 1979 that democratically elected councillors took office, a process that saw the decentralized management of Barcelona and its districts. The council deals with urban planning, transport, road maintenance and safety, the provision of sports facilities, libraries and public housing. It is also responsible for collecting the municipal tax to pay for these services.

PLAÇA DE SANT JUST

Barri Gòtic

One of the most renowned restaurants in Barcelona is the Café de l'Academia, tucked away in this small square. The square is dominated by the church of Saint Just, which has been on this site since the fourth century and which was used by the first archbishops of the city until the cathedral was built. The fountain in the square is reported to have been the first public drinking supply and is made from local Montjuïc stone that was carved in the late fourteenth century. The facial images are allegedly of Saint Just.

PLAÇA GEORGE ORWELL

Barri Gòtic

This square was named in honour of the English writer George Orwell (1903–50), who briefly served on the Republican side during the Spanish Civil War. He was a committed socialist and his writings up until then, including *Road to Wigan Pier*, were about social injustice. During the fighting, Orwell was wounded in the throat by a sniper's bullet, narrowly missing a vital artery. He was hospitalized and then became a wanted man when the political party he had joined in Spain (the communist Partido Obrero de Unificación Marxista) was declared illegal. On his return to England, he penned his memoir *Homage to Catalonia*.

PALAU DE LA MÚSICA CATALANA

La Ribera

The centrepiece of this magnificent auditorium is the
extraordinary stained-glass roof light. The concert hall was built
between 1905 and 1908 in the *Modernista* style to the design
of Lluís Domènech, one of the most prominent architects in
Catalonia. In 1997, after a major refurbishment, the building was
declared a UNESCO World Heritage Site. All of the decoration,
both inside and out, is dedicated to music, and in particular,
the Catalan tradition. The hall, which seats over two thousand
people, was originally built for choral music recitals, but today
offers a much wider repertoire.

MERCAT DE SANTA CATERINA

La Ribera

The market takes its name from a former convent on this
site, closed down as part of the secularization programme
of ecclesiastical buildings in the 1830s. It was replaced by a
covered market in 1845 and has continued to thrive to this
day. In 2005, a complete refurbishment of the space was
undertaken and a new multicoloured roof was added as part
of the scheme. The roof is supported on the front elevation by
slender twisted steel girders resembling trees, which give the
building an organic form.

BAR DEL CONVENT

La Ribera

Unlike many other ecclesiastical buildings, the Convent de
Sant Agustí was not desecrated during the nineteenth century,
since this one had been appropriated by the military after it was
partially destroyed during the Siege of Barcelona in 1714. The
buildings were still being used until the time of the Spanish
Civil War, when they fell into disrepair. Today, the cloister area
has been turned into a bar, where one can relax in the shade of
this medieval building. Another draw to this area is the chocolate
museum (Museu de la Xocolata), a favourite with the tourists.

MUSEU PICASSO

La Ribera

When it opened in 1963, this was the first museum in the world dedicated to Pablo Picasso and was the only one opened in the artist's lifetime. It boasts over 4,000 works by Picasso, and is considered by many to be the most comprehensive permanent collection of his work. Although born in southern Spain, Picasso always had a stronger affinity with Catalonia and Barcelona. The museum and primary collection were given by a friend of Picasso, Jaume Sabartés (1881–1968), a Catalan who acted as his administrator. There is a square nearby that is named in Sabartés' honour (Plaça Sabartés).

PALAU DEL MARQUÈS DE LIÓ

La Ribera

The Design Museum of Barcelona is based in the Poblenou area of the city in its headquarters at the Disseny Hub (*see* page 180). There is also another venue at the Palau del Marquès de Lió in the Old Town. This location is the archive or reference centre, and it is also used as a temporary exhibition space. When it was opened in 1969, it housed the Textile and Clothing Museum, but now hosts the Museum of Cultures of the World.

STREETS

El Born

A tiny enclave of the Ribera district, El Born was once the venue for medieval jousts. Today, it is home to a plethora of shops, boutiques and galleries selling high-end merchandise on the larger streets, such as Passeig del Born. In the narrow streets fanning out from the Mercat del Born, one can find many cafés and bars, which can be quite raucous at times. There is also a textile museum here, since traditionally, this was where the trade was located.

MERCAT DEL BORN

El Born

This market is the largest covered square in Europe, its design in iron and glass being the first of its kind in Barcelona, marking the beginnings of architectural Modernism in the city. It was opened for business in 1878 and was the main market in the city after 1921, until its closure in 1971. Currently, it is used as a museum and cultural centre. The building is located on the site of the former Ciutadella military garrison, parts of which are now revealed in the central hall of the building.

BOOMTOWN
BARCELONA

Developed in the nineteenth century as an expansion of the city centre, the Eixample is the district that is home to most of the *Modernista* architecture of Barcelona. Much of this is located in the Quadrat d'Or (Golden Square), but the centrepiece is Gaudí's Sagrada Família church. The district is laid out in a strict grid pattern of squares, but the corners of each intersection are chamfered to allow for vistas. The exceptions to the squared geometry are two diagonal roads running north–south and east–west. One of these is the Avinguda Gaudí that runs from the Sagrada Família to the Hospital de la Santa Cruz i San Pau; the other, which is nearly seven miles long, is the Avinguda Diagonal, which begins in the western district of Les Corts and ends at the Parc del Forum in Sant Martí to the east, dissecting part of the Eixample district en route.

Some of the *Modernista* buildings in the district are no longer used for their original purposes and have been appropriated by various organizations and businesses. One such is a house designed in 1880, the first in the city to use iron in its construction, that is now home to the Fundació Antoni Tàpies.

HOSPITAL DE LA SANTA CRUZ I SAN PAU

Eixample

Named after the old hospital and the benefactor of the new, Pau Gil (1816–96), this building is one of the most extraordinary examples of Catalan Modernism and Art Nouveau. It was designed by Lluís Domènech and constructed between 1902 and 1930, overseen firstly by the original architect and then by his son Pere (1881–1962). In total, there are 19 buildings in the complex, although the main entrance and façade are by far the most striking. The complex is a UNESCO World Heritage Site.

INTERIOR, HOSPITAL DE LA SANTA CRUZ I SAN PAU

Eixample

The opulence of the exterior is surpassed on the inside of this remarkable building. Its colourfu, airy interior was intended as a counter to the traditionally gloomy hospital atmposhere that often had an adverse effect on the patients. It is a strange, eclectic mix of Gothic and Byzantine styling infused with a Moorish heritage and elements of the Rococo. Since 2014, the building and its interior have been open to the public so everyone can enjoy this colourful masterpiece.

BASILICA OF THE SAGRADA FAMÍLIA

Eixample

Arguably the most famous building in Barcelona, it is considered the masterpiece of its architect, Antoni Gaudí. It was conceived in 1882, with Gaudí taking over the following year and radically changing the design. The church was never going to be completed in Gaudí's lifetime, because of the complexity of the design and its construction that relies on an organic evolution. When Gaudí died in 1926, less than a quarter of his vision was realized, and today, it is still incomplete. It was, however, made a minor basilica by Pope Benedict XIV (b. 1927) in 2010.

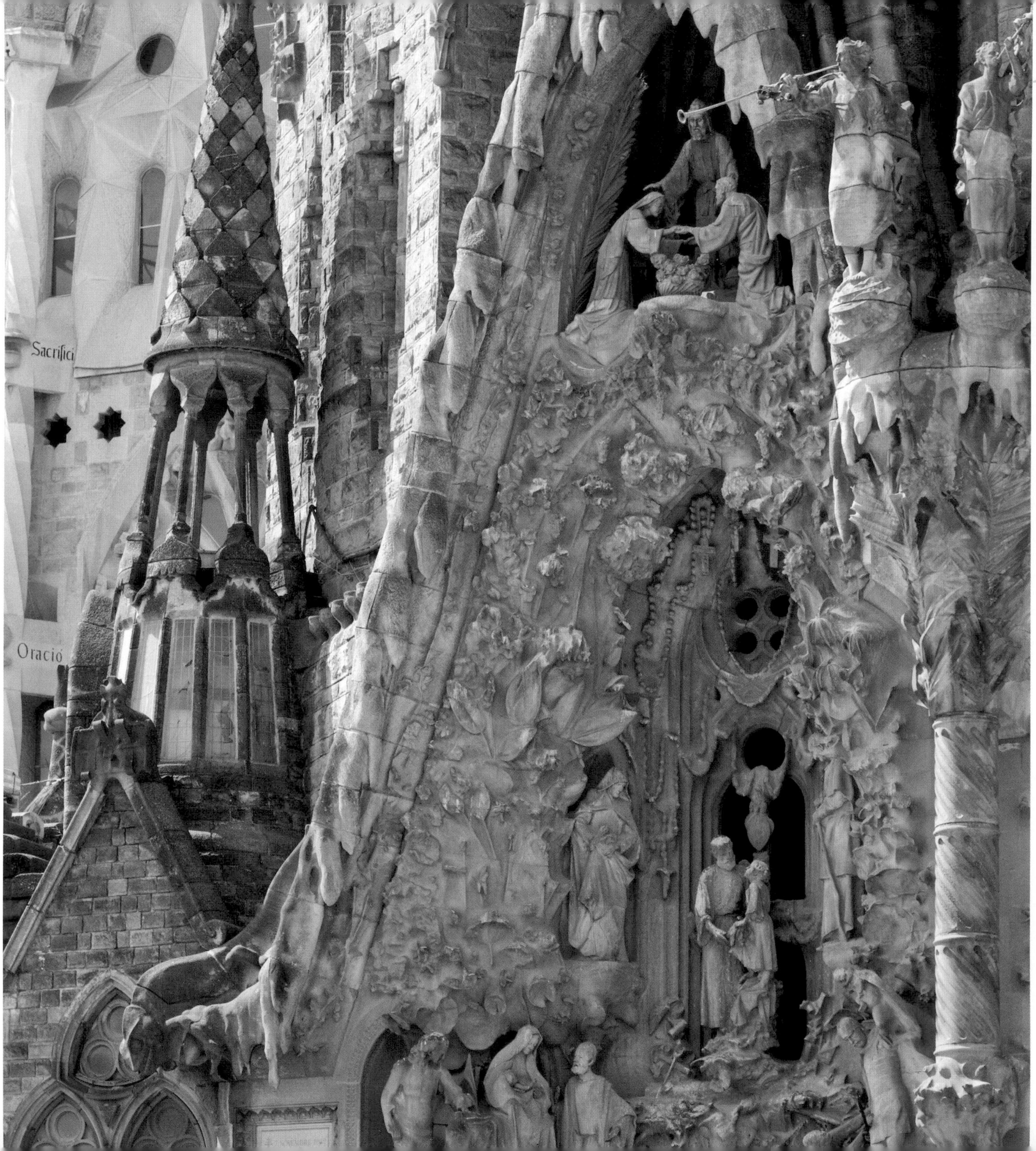
Sacrifici
Oració

FAÇADE, BASILICA OF THE SAGRADA FAMÍLIA

Eixample

The development of the church was interrupted during the Spanish Civil War, when a group of anarchists badly damaged the structure, as well as Gaudí's models and his workshop. Since 1940, the work has continued, but has been adapted and reinterpreted by later architects following the destruction of the original drawings. Modern technologies have enabled a faster design and construction process, but it is not anticipated that completion will be before 2026, the centenary of Gaudí's death.

CASA DE LES PUNXES

Eixample

A contemporary of Gaudí was another Modernist architect, Josep Puig i Cadafalch, who designed the Casa de les Punxes for the then President of FC Barcelona, Bartomeu Terradas (1874–1948). He, along with his three sisters, had inherited the family fortune from their industrialist father, also called Bartomeu (1846–1901). The home was for his sisters and mother and begun in 1905. Although considered a *Modernista* building, it resembles a medieval castle on the outside, while the interiors are lavished with stained glass and other polychromatic features akin to those of the Art Nouveau style.

FAÇADE, PALAU DEL BARÓ DE QUADRAS

Eixample

Another house that Puig i Cadafalch worked on at the same time was the nearby Palau del Baró de Quadras, a small *Modernista* building with two very different façades: one is neo-Gothic and would not look out of place in Venice; the other, at the rear of the property, is a *Modernista* town house with Art Nouveau detailing. The interior is a wonderful infusion of these two styles that borrows heavily from Moorish motifs, particularly in the foyer and Diagonal Room. Perhaps the most unusual interior feature is the Rosselló Room's fireplace.

STAIRCASE, PALAU DEL BARÓ DE QUADRAS

Eixample

The staircase of the house is a tour de force, an eclectic mix of styles that relies heavily on Moorish antecedents. The stairwell is lit from above through an ornately decorated glass panel to create a bright atrium. This in turn illuminates the golden ceramic tiles and highlights the decorative fountain at its centre. The building is currently used as the offices of the Institut Ramon Llull, an organization that promotes the Catalan language.

CASA COMALAT

Eixample

At first glance, especially if viewed from the rear, this building would appear to be the work of Gaudí, but is in fact by another *Modernista* architect, Salvador Valeri (1873–1954). It is set close by the Palau del Baró de Quadras and, like it, has two very different façades. The front is in coloured stone and is organic in form, adhering very much to the curvilinear forms of Art Nouveau and is almost neo-Rococo. The rear is somewhat at odds with it, a riot of colour adorned with ceramics, redolent of Gaudí's work.

MERCAT DE LA CONCEPCIÓ

Eixample

The market takes its name from the nearby Church of the Immaculate Conception, and has been in existence since 1888. Aside from the usual offerings of meat, fish and vegetables, this market has a large area dedicated to flowers, herbs and succulents. Incredibly, this section of the market is open 24 hours a day and 365 days of the year. The market is also a hub for the community to meet and socialize.

PALAU MACAYA

Eixample

Romàn Macaya Gibert (1843–1923), a wealthy industrialist, commissioned Puig i Cadafalch to design a new family home for him in what is now the Eixample district of Barcelona. Work began in 1898 and the house was completed in 1901, the family living there until 1914. Puig i Cadafalch used the finest artisans for the ornamentation, including sculptors Eusebi Arnau (1864–1933) for the doorways and stone balcony decorations, and Alfons Juyol (1860–1917), who had also worked on the Baró de Quadras. The building was acquired by La Caixa in 1947 and is now a cultural centre, EspaiCaixa.

FAÇADE, CASA MILÀ

Eixample

It is easy to imagine the controversy caused by the design and construction of the Casa Milà or, as it came to be known pejoratively, La Pedera, which means 'stone quarry'. The building, which has no straight lines, is an extreme example of using the curvilinear forms of Art Nouveau in the building's construction rather than just its decoration. The architect was Antoni Gaudí, who sought to express his ideas of a free surface area, rather than following the geometry of a conventional building. This block of apartments was begun in 1905 and finished in 1910.

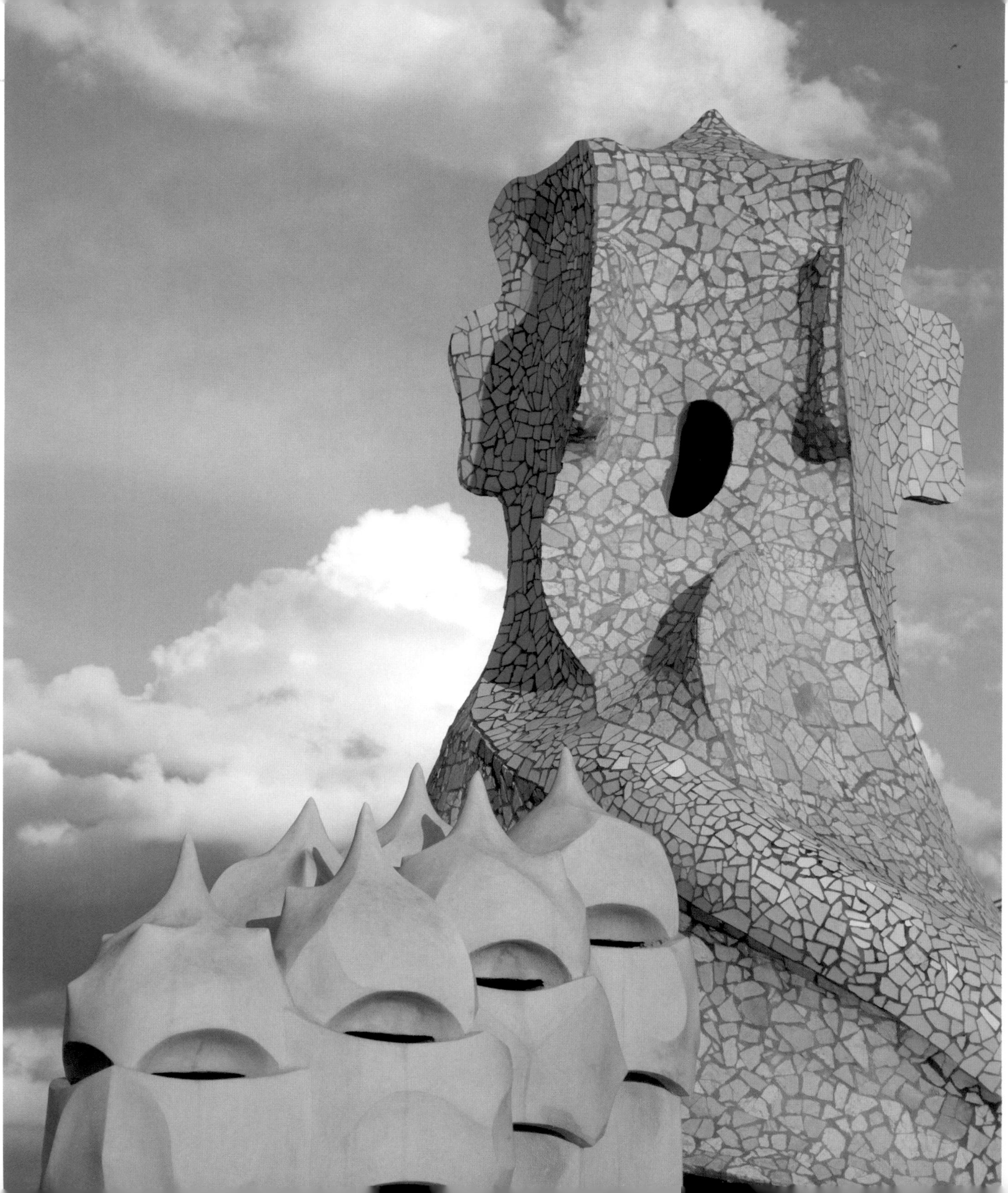

CHIMNEYS, CASA MILÀ

Eixample

A notable element of the building, beyond its organic shape, is the decorative rooftop. The roof has a number of utilitarian items such as skylights, fans and chimneys, which are all made of brick and then covered in additional elements such as broken marble and glass. The roof is home to what appears to be a sculpture garden, such is the diversity of shape and decoration. Another aspect of the apartment block is that Gaudí designed much of the interior furniture.

PASSEIG DE GRÀCIA

Eixample

Regarded as the most expensive street in Barcelona, the wide boulevard of the Passeig de Gràcia was originally a rural lane outside of central Barcelona, but with the expansion of the Eixample district, it had became very fashionable by the end of the nineteenth century. Several of the *Modernista* architects were commissioned to design buildings along this road, most notably Gaudí and his Casa Milà. Today, the most innovative architects are still designing buildings for this street, most recently the Wave Building by Toyo Ito (b. 1941) in 2009.

STREET LAMPS, PASSEIG DE GRÀCIA

Eixample

This fashionable street has a number of unique benches and street lanterns designed by Pere Falqués (1850–1916). Falqués was a Modernist architect and designed the Palace of Sciences and Agriculture at the Barcelona World's Fair of 1888. For the Passeig de Gràcia commission, executed in 1906, the 32 lanterns overhang the wide boulevard and adopt the sinuous lines of Art Nouveau styling for the decoration. The benches were decorated using mosaic work, a style that often causes the work to be wrongly attributed to Gaudí.

FUNDACIÓ ANTONI TÀPIES

Eixample

The Catalan Antoni Tàpies (1923–2012) was one of the foremost European artists of the mid-twentieth century. He was associated with the movement known as *Art Informel*, an approach to abstract painting that had an improvisatory and gestural technique that was more to do with the materiality of the paint than of subject matter. Tàpies was one of a small number of artists to have created a public museum dedicated to his work and those of his contemporaries. It was opened in 1990 in a building designed by the *Modernista* architect Lluís Domènech in 1880.

CHIMNEYS, CASA BATLLÓ

Eixample

The nickname for the building is the Casa dels Ossos (House of Bones) because of its skeletal quality. The house has a curved roof and is often likened to a dragon's back and, as with most of Gaudí's work, is decorated in mosaic, in this case to represent the dragon's scales. The chimneys shown here, as well as being highly decorative, are also functional, as they are designed to prevent backdrafts. Linking the roof to the façade is an elaborate spire with a cross on top, a symbol of Gaudí's profound religious faith.

FAÇADE, CASA BATLLÓ

Eixample

On the most prestigious street in Barcelona, the Passeig de Gràcia, three of the most prominent *Modernista* architects competed to redesign three existing separate houses in a block that became known as La Manzana de la Discordia. Since *manzana* means both 'block' and 'apple' in Spanish, it was a reference to the 'Apple of Discord' in Greek mythology. The critics were referencing the diverse approaches to *Modernista* by the three architects in this scheme. By far and away the most flamboyant of these is Gaudí's Casa Batlló.

CASA AMATLLER

Eixample

Another contributor to La Manzana de la Discordia was the architect Puig i Cadafalch, who created the Casa Amatller for the chocolatier Antoni Amatller (1851–1910). Amatller, a wealthy businessman who had established the largest chocolate factory in Spain at the time, was a generous patron of the arts and owned a large collection of paintings. These can be seen at the house today, courtesy of the Fundació Institut Amatller, set up by his daughter. The Casa Amatller was completed in 1900, its stepped façade heavily decorated with ornamentation by Eusebi Arnau.

CASA LLEÓ MORERA

Eixample

The least eccentric but equally flamboyant of the trio is the Casa Lleó Morera, on the corner at the junction with Carrer del Consell de Cent. One of the most striking elements of the façade is the tempietto (a small, temple-like decoration) at the top, recently restored after damage sustained during the Spanish Civil War. The design is by Lluís Domènech and, as with other *Modernista* architects, he collaborated with different artisans to create a 'total work of art'. The sculptor Eusebi Arnau carved a number of mulberry tree rebuses into the façade; *morera* translates as 'mulberry' in English.

CASA ANTONI ROCAMORA

Eixample

A much lesser known architect of *Modernista* is Bonaventura Bassegoda (1862–1940), who worked with his brother Joachim (1854–1938) to create the Casa Antoni Rocamora on the Passeig de Gràcia in 1914. The building is based more on Venetian Gothic, with its projecting windows, and has none of the excesses associated with his contemporaries such as Gaudí. The most notable features of the building are the two domed flanking towers and the elaborate central tower with the gold tiled roof. The grandson of Bonaventura Bassegoda, Juan (1930-2012), was a leading expert on the work of Gaudí.

PLAZA MONUMENTAL DE BARCELONA

Eixample

When the new bullring was commissioned in 1911, a different approach was used, one that was specifically anti-Modernist. This style, which came to be known as *Nuocentista,* sought more discipline in design and construction. The bullring's original design was, however, altered slightly when a disciple of Gaudí, Domènec Sugrañes (1878–1938) finished the work, adding much to the decorative façade. The bullring was in use up until 2012, when a ban on bullfighting imposed by the Catalan authorities came into effect.

TALLER MASRIERA

Eixample

Known as the Masriera Workshop, this elaborate Greek Revival building was made for the brothers José (1841–1912) and Francesc Masriera (1842–1902), who were renowned artists and goldsmiths. It was designed by Josep Vilaseca, already Professor of Architecture at the Barcelona School of Architecture when he accepted this commission in 1882. When Francesc died his son Lluís (1872–1958), himself a renowned jewellery designer, took over the premises, and in 1932, added a small theatre for the performing arts.

CAN BATLLÓ

Eixample

Another example of the *Nuocentista* style of architecture can be found at the old industrial school building, part of the Can Batlló industrial complex created by the Batlló family as a facility for their huge textile empire. In contrast to the Casa Batlló by Gaudí, the school is altogether more disciplined and ordered in its pragmatic design by Joan Rubió (1870–1952), who was actually a pupil of Gaudí. There are a number of other buildings in the complex, most notably the Clock Building, that were appropriated as small artisanal workshops after the closure of the factory.

SOUTHERN AND WESTERN BARCELONA

T**he focus of this section is Montjuïc, a hill that rises to 213 m (700 ft) and overlooks the waterfront. The location was used for the 1929 World Fair, when the Palau Nacional was built high up on the hill, with terracing down to the Plaça d'Espanya with its centrepiece, the Magic Fountain. Further up the hill is the Castell de Montjuïc, and close by is the Olympic Stadium, originally built for the 1936 Summer Games, which were cancelled due to the outbreak of the Spanish Civil War. The stadium was revamped and enlarged for the 1992 Games.**

The Les Corts area is the home of Barcelona Football Club, one of the most successful clubs in Europe, having won Spain's La Liga 25 times and 20 European titles. The club is consistently one of the top three wealthiest clubs worldwide.

The Pedralbes area is one of the most sought-after areas of Barcelona for property, since many wealthy industrialists and businessmen commissioned the building of their own fine homes here in the late nineteenth and early twentieth centuries.

MERCAT DE SANT ANTONI

Sant Antoni

Opened in 1882, the market was created to provide produce for the locals of Sant Antoni, located between the neighbourhoods of El Raval and Montjüic. The market building had been closed for a while for refurbishment, but is now open again, a splendid example of wrought-iron and glass architecture. The octagonal dome is functional, since it forms the outer perimeter corridors that separate the various other areas, selling clothing, books and objets d'art. Certain days of the week are allocated for the sale of these items at the market.

STREET ART

Sant Antoni

Like most major cities in Europe, the phenomenon of street art has become prevalent in certain areas of Barcelona. Of course, like Paris and London, the city is famed for several avant-garde artists in the twentieth century and their legacy lives on through street art. One of the best known of these is El Xupet Negre (The Black Pacifier), whose trademark is a logo of a infant's dummy. Like his English equivalent Banksy, he remains anonymous. The piece shown here is also anonymous and appeared on a house used by squatters in Sant Antoni.

MONTJUÏC CEMETERY

Montjuïc

Due to the industrialization of the city in the 1900s, the population almost trebled in the last 40 years of the century. Consequently, the old cemetery at Poblenou (*see* page 000) had reached capacity. A new facility was opened in 1883, on the rocky slopes of Montjuïc. Its winding paths and terracing provide outstanding views towards the Mediterranean. Currently there are over a million burials and interments within the 23 ha (57 acre) site. One notable interment here is of the artist Joan Miró.

CAIXAFORUM

Montjuïc

Resembling a huge castle, this building was in fact a factory designed by Josep Puig i Cadafalch for the Casaramona Company, that made blankets and towels, to replace their earlier building destroyed in a fire. It opened in 1913 amid much acclaim, but the company ran into financial difficulties and closed its doors for the last time in 1920. Until 1992, the police used the building for stabling, but it was then bought by the financial institution La Caixa for their foundation to create a cultural centre, its present purpose.

BARCELONA PAVILION

Montjuïc

The original pavilion, of which this is a 1987 reconstruction, was commissioned by the German government for the Barcelona Exposition of 1929. Resembling a private villa, it functioned as a reception area for dignitaries – the chairs were designed for the king and queen of Spain – and as a retreat from the summer heat for visitors. It was designed on a radical open plan, to ensure both light and a free flow of space, and continues to be a source of inspiration to many architects.

MUSEU NACIONAL D'ART DE CATALUNYA

Montjuïc

A magnificent building originally used as the centrepiece for the 1929 Exposition, since 1934, it has housed the main collection of Catalan art and has been extended to facilitate its growing collection. A major part of that collection is the Romanesque and Gothic artefacts, unrivalled in the world, focussing in particular on the medieval territories of Aragon, Navarre and Castile. Although centring on Catalan art, the museum also has many works by leading Spanish artists, such as El Greco, Goya and Velàsquez. It also houses the large Cambó collection of fine art.

MAGIC FOUNTAIN

Montjuïc

The Museu Nacional is best seen at night, when illuminated and with water cascading down either side through the steps and the fountains are lit. Designed by Carles Buïgas (1898–1979), who described his creations as *aqualuz* ('watery light'), the Magic Fountain of Montjuïc is his masterpiece. It was a phenomenal success at the 1929 Exposition, but was badly damaged during the Spanish Civil War and did not work again until 1955. The 1992 Olympic Games saw the fountains completely restored and brought into use for the opening ceremony.

FUNDACIÓ JOAN MIRÓ

Montjuïc

Miró set up his own foundation in 1968 to create a workshop and gallery space for young contemporary artists. With his friend Joan Prats (1891–1970), an artist and promoter, he established the space that has now become the Fundació Joan Miró, Centre d'Estudis d'Art Contemporani, which opened its doors in 1975. The austere Modernist building was designed by Josep Lluís Sert (1902–83). Today, the museum has a permanent collection of work by Miró, Tàpies and René Magritte (1898–1967), the Belgian Surrealist, as well as providing exhibition space for contemporary artists.

PALAU SANT JORDI ARENA

Montjuïc

Created in 1992 for the Olympic Games as an indoor sporting arena, the Palau Sant Jordi now hosts not only sports events but concerts too. It has a seating capacity of nearly 18,000 and is the largest indoor arena in Spain. It was designed by the Japanese architect Arata Isozaki (b. 1931), who was also responsible for the new entranceway to the CaixaForum (*see* page 129). Close by the arena is the white Montjuïc communications tower, standing at 136 m (446 ft) tall, constructed for Telefónica to transmit coverage of the Barcelona Olympics.

CASTELL DE MONTJUÏC

Montjuïc

At the summit of Montjuïc is a former military fortress built in 1640. The fortress successfully defended the Catalans against Spanish authority in 1641. The garrison was less successful against the British during the War of Spanish Succession 50 years later. The castle was captured again during the Napoleonic Wars, but saw its most bloody conflicts between 1936 and 1939, when both sides in the Spanish Civil War used the facility for torture, imprisonment and execution. Today, the facility is controlled by the Barcelona City Council and is used as a municipal facility with gardens.

PARC DE MONTJUÏC

Montjuïc

To the north of the castle and linked to it by a funicular railway is the Parc de Montjuïc, high up on the hillside with spectacular views of Barcelona. The most breathtaking views are at the Mirador de l'Alcalde, which is laid out in a series of terraces. This pleasant walkway, with small water features and beautiful gardens, affords views of almost everything in Barcelona, most especially the harbours and across the Mediterranean. The other spectacular view from here is of the Museu Nacional d'Art de Catalunya and the Magic Fountain.

PARAL·LEL

El Poble-Sec

On the way down from Montjuïc by cable car to Paral·lel metro station, one can see the three tall chimneys of the former power station on the Avinguda del Paral·lel, now the offices of the utilities company Red Elèctrica d'Espanya that is responsible for Spain's national grid. Close by is the Three Chimneys Park, an urban space that contains a skate park and is also home to some of the most impressive street art in Barcelona. There are also several large outside sculptures made from the detritus of the old power station's interior.

STREETS

El Poble-Sec

South of the Avinguda del Paral·lel, and away from the large cabaret bars and theatres of the district, is the relatively quieter area known as El Poble-Sec. Here, there is a plethora of tapas bars and other restaurants, as well as a residential area. Its unusual name means 'dry town' and was in fact the last district in Barcelona to have running water provided. For the visitor, this offers a calm oasis, its shaded squares and tree-lined streets providing sanctuary from the hustle and bustle of the downtown areas.

PARC DE JOAN MIRÓ

Sants

On the site of a former municipal slaughterhouse, the authorities decided in 1979 to build a new recreational space as part of a new post-Franco Barcelona. The result was the large urban space known as the Parc de Joan Miró, one of the foremost names in Catalan culture. This was one of many similar projects that followed, addressing current social needs but also in a bid to renew Catalan culture, so long repressed by Franco's regime. The focal point of the park is the 22 m (72 ft)-high sculpture *Dona i Ocell* (Woman and Bird) by Miró.

PARC DE L'ESPANYA INDUSTRIAL

Sants

Another former commercial space reclaimed by the authorities for use as a leisure area is the Parc de l'Espayna Industrial, opened in 1985 to designs by the Basque architect Luis Peña Ganchegui (1926–2009). In the centre of the park is a large man-made lake. One of the features in the park is the huge dragon sculpture by Andrés Nagel (b. 1947), which doubles as a slide for children. This is complemented by a number of other public sculptures used at the 1929 Exposition, thereafter kept in storage.

CAMP NOU

Les Corts

With a seating capacity of almost 100,000, the Camp Nou football stadium is the largest of its kind in Europe. It was opened in 1957 and replaced the old stadium in the same location. Apart from being the home ground of FC Barcelona, it has also been used for several European Cup finals and was one of the venues for the 1982 FIFA World Cup. The stadium has been further developed in recent years and is also used for concerts, including one by the Three Tenors.

PARC DE CERVANTES

Les Corts

In the west of the city is the area known as Pedralbes, where there is a green space dedicated to Spain's greatest writer, Cervantes. Its location is just north of the eastern end of the Avinguda Diagonal, a wide boulevard of some 11 km (6.8 miles) in length. The park is approximately 9 ha (22 acres) in size and is predominantly open, grassy areas, but there is also a magnificent rose garden of some 4 ha (10 acres) that has many species to provide almost year-round colour. The park has also hosted the International Rose Show.

AVINGUDA DE PEDRALBES

Pedralbes

Another busy thoroughfare is the Avinguda de Pedralbes, which runs almost at right angles to the Avinguda Diagonal but is considerably shorter. Many of the Modernist homes built in the early twentieth century have long disappeared and been replaced by more traditional plain apartment blocks. There are, however, a handful of the originals left along this expensive strip to remind us of its past glories. Pedralbes, which is Catalan for 'white stones', is home to a former monastery that is made from this stone and is now a museum.

PALAU REIAL DE PEDRALBES

Pedralbes

Eusebi Güell acquired the land on which the original seventeenth-century house stood, amounting to some 30,000 sq m (323,000 sq ft), in 1872. Güell was made a count by King Alfonso XIII (1886–1941) in 1908, and in gratitude, he gave the original house and some of the land to the royal family, who then converted it into a small palace for their use while in the city. When the second republic was formed in 1931, the city government acquired the palace, but during Franco's regime, it was used by the dictator as a residence. Today, it is the home of the Museu de Ceramica.

PAVELLONS DE LA FINCA GÜELL

Pedralbes

In 1884, Gaudí was commissioned by his patron Eusebi Güell to remodel another house on his estate at Pedralbes. The house had been constructed some years earlier to designs by Gaudí's teacher Joan Martorell (1833–1906). Gaudí's plan was to create a series of pavilions based on an Orientalist theme, popular in Europe at the time. However, Gaudí's designs were based on Moorish motifs that could be found in medieval Aragon. The complex is enclosed by a wall and gates, one of which has an extraordinary stylized dragon incorporated into its design.

CLOISTER OF THE MONESTIR DE SANTA MARIA DE PEDRALBES

Pedralbes

Considered the world's largest Gothic cloister, the three-storey fourteenth-century building is the heart of the monastery. It was founded by the monarchy and the capitals at the top of the columns of the cloister bear their coats of arms. It was run by the Poor Nuns of St Clare until quite recently, although their history there has been a chequered one, having been expelled at least twice in their 700-year history. Today, the old monastery is used as a museum and the nuns live in a new convent adjoining the old buildings.

CARRER MAJOR DE SARRIÀ

Sarrià-Sant Gervasi

One of the largest districts outside of central Barcelona is Sarrià-Sant Gervasi, which lies to the north. It became part of the city in 1921, but its narrow streets and small houses still give it a small village atmosphere. The main street is the Carrer Major, with its shops, offices and of course a market. Opposite the market is the church of San Vicente, a beautiful Baroque interior encased in a much older Romanesque exterior from the twelfth century, with several modifications since.

CAN PONSIC

Sarrià-Sant Gervasi

This castle-like structure was reconstructed from an earlier building, some parts thought to be from as early as the eleventh-century, by the architect Augusto Font (1846–1924). The work was completed in 1892, for the aristocratic Ponsich family, its last owner being Josep Ponsich (1892–1982). Today, it is owned by Barcelona City Council and is used as the home of the Urban Guard, the local police force, whose uniform is very similar to that of London's Metropolitan Force.

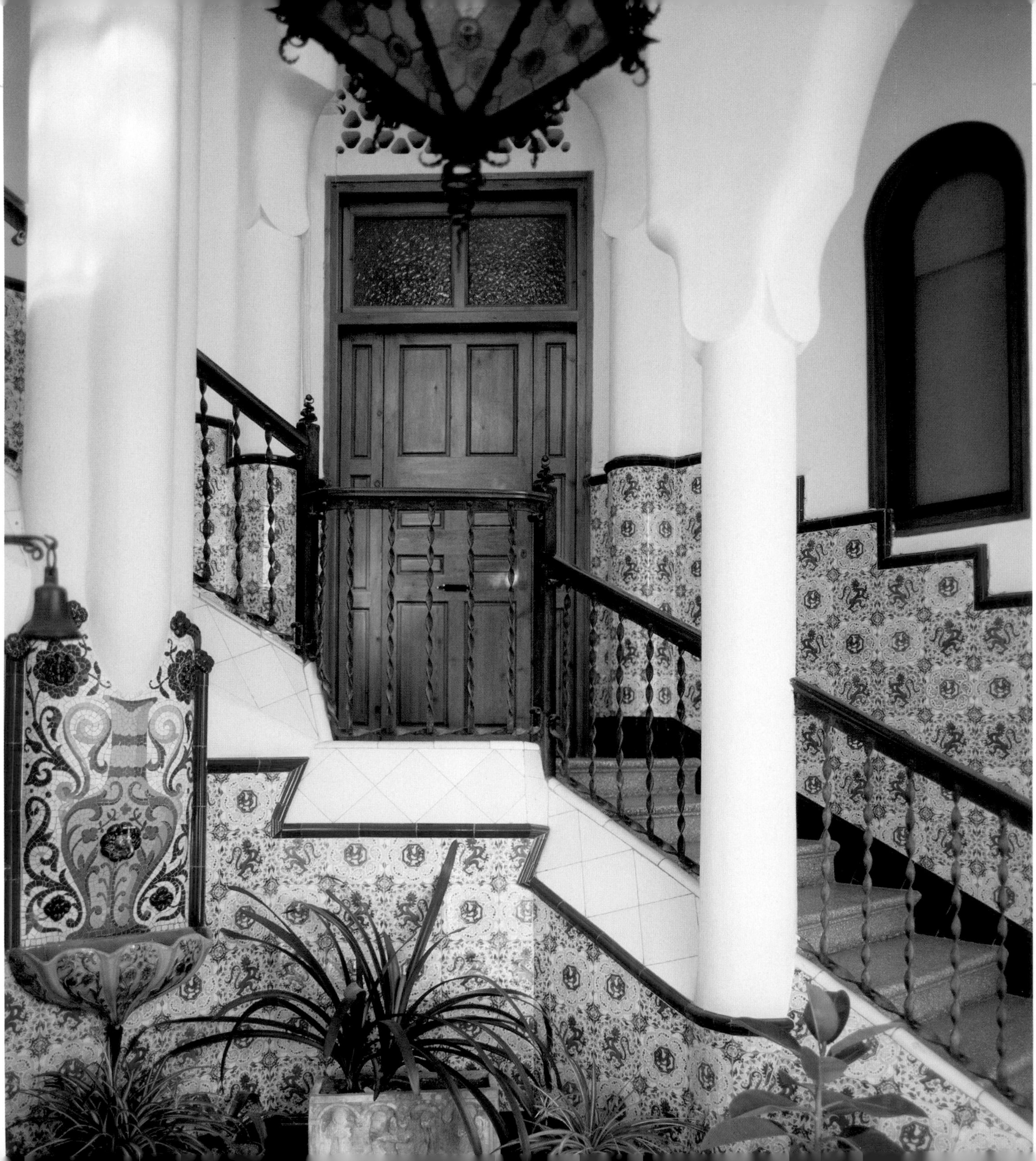

INTERIOR, BELLESGUARD TOWER

Sarrià-Sant Gervasi

Built between 1900 and 1909 is a rather extraordinary manor house designed by Antoni Gaudí for the Figueras family. There was originally a ruined castle on the site, built for the King of Aragon in the fifteenth century. Gaudí retained the remaining walls and its medieval heritage in the new build, which is quite austere on the outside compared to many of his other houses. However, the interior is as ostentatious as might be expected. Unfortunately, the Figueras family never lived in the house, but its subsequent owners enjoyed the magnificence for over 70 years.

COLLEGI DE LES TERESIANES

Sarrià-Sant Gervasi

This college and study facility for the Teresian Congregation had already begun laying out the footprint of the building when Gaudí was asked to take over the project in 1888. Within two years, he had completed this tour de force of the Catalan neo-Gothic style. Due to the restraints on budget, there is none of the exuberance normally associated with Gaudí, a devout Catholic who once stated that a church is the only thing worthy of representing the soul of a people. Nevertheless, one can still feel he excelled himself in this remarkable work.

COSMOCAIXA BARCELONA

Sarrià-Sant Gervasi

The main building occupied today by Barcelona's Science Museum was originally created between 1904 and 1909 by Josep Domènech in a *Modernista* style and served as housing for blind girls. The building was reconfigured and enlarged between 1979 and 1981 and opened to the public as the Caixa. The museum proved very popular and it was necessary to provide additional exhibition space and facilities. In 2004 the new museum was opened, becoming the CosmoCaixa.

VALLVIDRERA RESERVOIR

Sarrià-Sant Gervasi

The community of Sarrià obtained its drinking water from the Vallvidrera Reservoir up until the beginning of the twentieth century. After several decades of being abandoned, it was eventually acquired by the local community and turned into a nature reserve for everyone to enjoy. It is a very popular spot for families to picnic and walk along the purpose-built pathways, through the wooded areas that provide shade on hot summer days.

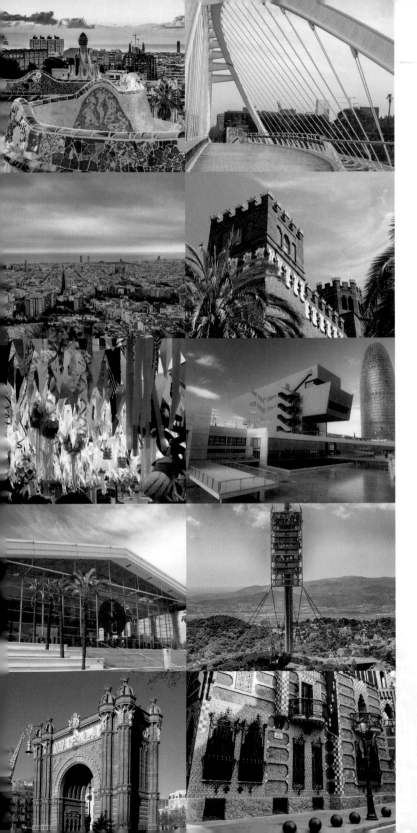

NORTHERN AND EASTERN BARCELONA

Gràcia is the smallest and most densely populated district of Barcelona after Eixample, which is on its southern border. The two districts are linked by the Passeig de Gràcia, but unlike the Eixample end of the boulevard, with its high-end, fashionable retail brands and five-star hotels, this end of the street is altogether more modest. Also unlike Eixample, there are very few tourist attractions in the area, making it an enclave of relatively quiet Catalan life, the residents proudly displaying their 'independent' flag.

The Tibidabo neighbourhood is perched high up at over 500 m (1,640 ft) above sea level and provides panoramic views of the city, particularly from the terrace of the Sacred Heart church at its summit.

El Poblenou, Catalan for 'new village', is on the north-eastern side of the city and part of its coastline. During the nineteenth century, this one-time separate municipality was at the heart of Spain's Industrial Revolution, the factories surrounded by working-class homes. As with so many other areas of Barcelona, this formerly down-at-heel neighbourhood was given a new lease of life for the Summer Olympics in 1992.

CASA VICENS

Gràcia

The first building designed by Gaudí was the Casa Vicens, and it is fitting that the house is now a museum dedicated to this seminal masterpiece. This was the house that took Gaudí on a journey throughout his career exploring Neo-Mudéjar motifs, a fusion of Catalan and Moorish styles that originated in late fifteenth-century Aragon. The commission by the Vicens family to build the house came before Gaudí had even graduated as an architect in 1878. Their trust was not misplaced, as the house heralded a new chapter in Catalan architecture.

FESTA MAJOR DE GRÀCIA

Gràcia

Every August, the streets (or barrio) around the Gràcia area of Barcelona come alive for a week-long festival as each street competes to win the coveted prize of 'Best Decorated'. It is fiercely competitive, as each creates its own theme and the prize is based on the most innovative and creative decoration. The festival is complemented with a number of concerts and outdoor shows. At the end of the festival week, there is a traditional *correfoc,* or 'fire run', in which fire-brandishing 'devils' run through the streets with flaming sparklers.

PARK GÜELL

Gràcia

Inspired by the English 'garden city' model at Letchworth, Count Güell imagined a similar Utopian ideal on his own land in Gràcia, an upland area with wonderful views, away from the smoky factories of Barcelona. Güell himself had a house already on the estate and commissioned the architect Francesc Berenguer (1866–1914) to build two show homes with a view to creating his

own 'garden city'. Unfortunately, it was a commercial failure with
no buyers. Gaudí was persuaded to buy one of the properties for
himself and his family, where they lived until 1926. The house is
now the Gaudí House Museum, opened in 1963.

MOSAIC DRAGON, PARK GÜELL

Gràcia

The landscaping of the grounds around Gaudí's house was commissioned by Güell and undertaken by the architect between 1900 and 1914. It was created during Gaudí's so-called naturalist phase, when he was inspired by the organic shapes and lines of nature. The focal point of the garden is the main terrace, accessed by a grand staircase. Part way up the staircase is a large mosaic dragon, with a fountain of water exiting through his open jaws. Park Güell is an extraordinary feat of innovative design, a wondrous spectacle of pure fantasy.

PARC DE LA CREUETA DEL COLL

Gràcia

Created as part of the city's de-urbanization plans in the 1970s, this area was previously a disused stone quarry and is now a leisure park. The large man-made lake is popular with bathers, as are the surrounding lawned areas for picnics. Suspended above a flooded part of the quarry is a huge 50-ton sculpture called *In Praise of Water* by the Basque artist Eduardo Chillida (1924–2002), based on the legend of Narcissus who fell in love with his own reflection. Around the lake are a number of other sculptures, such as *Totem* by Ellsworth Kelly (1923–2015).

TRAMVIA BLAU

Tibidabo

Despite the difficulty of getting to Tibidabo, at over 500 m (1,640 ft) above sea level, it offers the most spectacular view of Barcelona and across the Mediterranean Sea. Tibidabo is the tallest peak of the Serra de Collserola mountain range to the north of the city. The Tramvia Blau tramline, which dates from 1901, is a great way of getting to Tibidabo because it allows passengers to see many of the *Modernista* buildings en route.

TIBIDABO AMUSEMENT PARK

Tibidabo

A working amusement park since 1905, it was originally the idea of local businessman and entrepreneur Salvador Andreu (1841–1928). It is situated almost at the summit of Tibidabo, so the experience of a ride on the Ferris wheel enhances the views. The wheel is only one of 25 rides in the park, several of which are the originals from when the park first opened and are still in operation. One of the rides that opened in 1928 is the Avió aeroplane ride, which gives the impression of flying above the city.

TEMPLE EXPIATORI DEL SAGRAT COR

Tibidabo

At the very summit of Tibidabo is a church dedicated to the Sacred Heart of Jesus, designed by Enric Sagnier (1858–1931) and built between 1902 and 1961. The crypt resembles a Romanesque fortress, which is constructed in Montjuïc stone. Its interior is designed in a neo-Byzantine style. The main body of the church is altogether different, being neo-Gothic in design and using a much lighter-coloured stone. A bronze statue of Christ by Josep Miret (1907–44) crowns the top of the church.

TORRE DE COLLSEROLA

Tibidabo

Designed by the British architect Sir Norman Foster (b. 1935), the Tower of Collserola was created for the 1992 Olympic Games as a TV and radio transmitter. Support for the structure, which is made from reinforced concrete, is by guy wires. The highest antenna is nearly 304 m (1,000 ft) and in the centre is a pod with 13 floors that reaches to almost 152 m (500 ft). The tenth floor is open to the public as a viewing pod, where it is possible to gain one of the most spectacular views of the city.

TURÓ DE LA ROVIRA

Horta

At an altitude of 260 m (850 ft), the hill of the Turó de la Rovira provides spectacular views of Barcelona and the coastline. The hill has therefore always been occupied,

originally as a defensive position for the Romans and later as an anti-aircraft position during the Spanish Civil War. The bombardment of Barcelona in 1938 was the first large-scale aerial bombing of any city, and in order to defend it, several gun batteries were set up on high points, including this one.

ELS MISTOS

Horta

For the 1992 Olympic Games, a number of artworks were created for some of the urban spaces in Barcelona. In the main, they were light-hearted pieces intended to bring joy to the city, which had previously been an urban sprawl. One such commission was given to the American Pop artist Claes Oldenburg (b.1929) and his wife Coosje van Bruggen (1942–2009), who created *Els Mistos* (The Matches). As with most of their work, the banal and everyday objects have been enlarged and now stand as icons in the canon of modern art.

PARC DEL LABERINT D'HORTA

Horta

Set in the Horta-Guinardó district of Barcelona is a historical garden that has its origins in the eighteenth-century estate of Joan Antoni Desvalls i d'Ardena, the Marquis of Llupià, Poal and Alfarràs. The estate was given to the city in 1971, when it was first opened to the public. The park of about 8.9 ha (22 acres) is divided into the classical garden, which has two pavilions, and the romantic one, which has a waterfall. On the lower terrace of the former is a maze, which gave the park its name, made from trimmed cypress trees.

MIRADOR DE TORRÉ BARO

Nou Barris

Despite its medieval appearance, the castle of Torré Baro was actually constructed in the twentieth century. In fact, it has the look of a disused castle because it was designed to be a hotel and never completed. The name is taken from a much earlier fortress that stood on this site and was destroyed during the War of Spanish Succession in 1714. One is able to gain access to the rooftop of the building, which affords spectacular views across the city.

TORRÉ JULIA

Nou Barris

An entirely different tower in the same neighbourhood of Nou Barris is the Torré Julia, a 17-storey-high housing complex for the elderly. Its designers are Paul Vidal (b. 1977), Sergi Pons (b. 1977) and Richard Galiana (b. 1976), and the building was opened in 2012. It was specifically designed, unlike most housing blocks, to allow social interaction among the residents through the creation of very wide corridors and sun-shaded terraces. The project is part of the redevelopment of the Nou Barris district, which was originally a number of separate urban communities.

CASA BLOC

Sant Andreu

Adhering more to the conventional European Modernism of, for example, Le Corbusier is the Casa Bloc development in the Sant Andreu district of Barcelona. The architects were all members of the Catalan Group of Architects and Technicians for the Progress of Contemporary Architecture (GATCPAC) and included Josep Luis Sert. Like Le Corbusier, they sought a more humanitarian way of living that would improve workers' living conditions. The project was begun in 1932 and not completed before the outbreak of the Spanish Civil War in 1936.

BAC DE RODA BRIDGE

Sant Andreu

This bridge was constructed between 1984 and 1987 to improve the road infrastructure of Barcelona in preparation for the 1992 Summer Olympics, linking the districts of Sant Andreu and Sant Martí. Previously, the two districts were separated by railway lines, which the bridge straddles. The futuristic design was by the architect and structural designer Santiago Calatrava (b. 1951), who has also been responsible for the designs of Bilbao Airport (1990) and the Athens Olympic Sports Complex (2000–04). The bridge won Calatrava the 1987 FAD Architecture Prize.

MUSEU BLAU

Sant Martí

Located in the Forum Park near the waterfront, the Museu Blau is Barcelona's Natural History Museum. The triangular blue building that houses it was designed by the Swiss architecture firm Herzog and de Meuron, who were also responsible for the Tate Modern gallery in London. The 9,000 sq m (96,875 sq ft) building has a 3,000-seat auditorium, exhibition spaces and a restaurant, and its location, suspended above the ground, provides a covered plaza. The plaza is enhanced by the underside of the building and its reflective tiles that have the appearance of the sea.

PARC DIAGONAL MAR

Sant Martí

The museum is part of an urban renewal development, and was the main venue for the Forum Universal de les Cultures, hosted in 2004. Previously, this area was an urban wasteland with disused factories and warehouses. The Parc Diagonal Mar is so called because of its proximity to the end of the Avinguda Diagonal roadway. Although not a park in the strictest sense of the word, it is a regenerated 14 ha (35 acre) urban space divided into seven areas, each of which stimulates different sensations, the largest being the children's play area.

PLAÇA DE PRIM

Poblenou

Close by the Bar Bella beach is a former fishing village, now known as El Poblenou, or 'new village'. It is ideally located between the relaxing beach and the vast array of shops that have emerged following the regeneration of the area for the Olympics. Fortunately, the oldest square in the area, the Plaça de Prim, with its three ombú trees, is still as it was when it was created in the nineteenth century. In those days, it provided a meeting place for local fishermen; today, it offers a shady oasis for everyone.

TORRE AGBAR AND DISSENY HUB

Poblenou

An iconic symbol that punctuates the Barcelona skyline is the Agbar Tower, completed in 2005, one of several so-called hi-tech buildings in the city. The multi-occupancy building is used as offices, technical facilities and an auditorium. Around the tower is the Disseny Hub, a municipal facility that focuses on promoting the emerging design sector. A key element of the Disseny Hub is the Design Museum that is open to the public and provides information on the creative process.

MERCAT DEL ENCANTS

Poblenou

The largest and best known of Barcelona's flea markets is the Mercat del Encants (Market of Charms), situated in the Poblenou area. It has its roots in the late medieval period, but in 2013 the market was completely revamped, offering a covered market area and new facilities. The inside of the roof is made of polished zinc and provides a reflection of the market activity below. The market is open four days a week, with the busiest day being Saturday.

TEATRE NACIONAL DE CATALUNYA

Poblenou

The postmodern architect Ricardo Bofill (b. 1939), who also designed the W Barcelona hotel in Barceloneta, created the Teatre Nacional de Catalunya, which was completed in 1996. Since this is a cultural space, the architect has cleverly used the remains of another, the Parthenon in Athens, as his starting point. All that remains of the ancient monument are the outside Doric columns that enclose an empty space. Bofill has paid deference to this and enclosed the theatre space using glass rather than conventional building materials.

ARC DE TRIOMF

Poblenou

Built for the 1888 Barcelona World Fair, the triumphal arch provided the main access gate to the exhibition in the Ciutadella Park. It was designed by the Catalan architect Josep Vilaseca, a minor figure in the *Modernista* movement, that marked the evolution of Neoclassicism into *Modernisme*. The frieze at the top of the arch is called *Barcelona rep les nacions* (Barcelona welcomes the nations) and is by the sculptor Josep Reynés (1850–1926). Other friezes include allegories of agriculture, industry, trade and art, and are by other artists.

L'ESTACIÓ DEL NORD

Poblenou

Originally opened as a railway station in 1862, the building was closed exactly one hundred years later, with trains being diverted to other stations, including the Estació de França (*see* page 32). The building was acquired by the city council, and in 1983, work began on a refurbishment programme that would create a multipurpose sports hall, first used in 1992 as a venue for the Summer Olympics. Parts of the building are also used as a bus station and a police station.

CASTELL DELS TRES DRAGONS, PARC DE LA CIUTADELLA

Poblenou

Ciutadella is Catalan for citadel, and it was here in 1715 that a fortress was erected by King Philip V of Spain to suppress Catalan insurrections. The citadel became a hated symbol of oppression, and in the mid-nineteenth century was demolished by the city authorities, becoming Barcelona's only green space for several decades. Close to the entrance of the park is the Castell dels Tres Dragons. Initially built as a restaurant for the Exposition of 1888, it is now home to the Museum of Zoology.

DIPÒSIT DE LES AIGÜES

Poblenou

Originally designed by architect Josep Fontserè (1829–97), this former water tower was built to provide water for the fountains. It was modelled on large Roman reservoirs and built with the assistance of Gaudí, who was a student at the time. The tower has now been converted into a library for the Universitat Pompeu Fabra, Barcelona's newest public university created in 1990. The conversion of the tower was completed in 1999 to the designs of Lluís Clotet (b. 1941) and Ignacio Paricio (b. 1944), who have collaborated on many urban regeneration projects.

UMBRACLE, PARC DE LA CIUTADELLA

Poblenou

Close to the Zoology Museum is a winter pavilion and
a greenhouse, with the Geology Museum in between.
Together they make up the Museum of Natural Sciences. To
complement this there is also the Zoological Gardens, with a
collection of over 4,000 animals making it one of the largest in
Europe. Within the park area is also the former arsenal building
of the fortress, an elegant French classical building currently
used by the Parliament of Catalonia. There is also a very
elaborate fountain and cascade in the park designed by Josep
Fontserè.

INDEX